"Luke Laffin's *Reclaiming Your Core: Restoring the Foundations of Faith* is both timely and essential for the body of Christ and the season we are approaching. As I travel abroad teaching truth, I often find that many believers have lost the simplicity of the gospel. Luke presents this truth in a way that connects the believer back to the essential understanding of who we are, who He is, and the glorious truth of scripture.

I believe we are standing on the precipice of the most glorious days of human history as God continues to reveal who He is. With that being said, we face great challenges as winds of doctrine blow, attempting to disengage the believer from the Word. Go on this journey with Luke, and you'll find yourself shored up, equipped to run the race before you!"

—Dr. Jacob Biswell, JBM International

"This book is pure GOLD. It's well-balanced with real truth, grace, and love. Every believer needs to read and reread it throughout his/her journey.

It also took me into some past emotions and hurts that God needed me to revisit so I could receive a deeper level of healing and freedom. I am truly honored to have had the privilege to pre-read this book."

—Lonnie L. Ellis, author and founder of DRMI
(Damascus Road Ministries Int'l)

Reclaiming Your Core

Reclaiming Your Core

RESTORING THE FOUNDATIONS OF FAITH

Luke Laffin

Four Winds Global Foundation

ISBN: 0997810416
ISBN 978-0-9978104-0-0
ISBN 9780997810417

Published in the United States of America by
Four Winds Global Foundation
PO Box 99
Rancho Cordova, CA 95741

Cover Design: Luke Laffin
Cover Graphic Production: Luke Laffin and Jae Gravley

Book Developmental Editing/Consulting/Manuscript Editing:
AnnCastro Studio with Ann Castro, Katrina Ann Martin, Jae Gravley

Scripture quotations taken from the New American Standard Bible® (NASB). Copyright 1960, 1962, 1963, 1968, 1971, 1972, 1973, 1975, 1977, 1995 by The Lockman Foundation. Used by permission. www.Lockman.org

Glossary segments taken from Strong's Exhaustive Concordance of the Bible. Copyright 1990 by Thomas Nelson Publishers.

Printed in the United States of America by
CREATESPACE, an Amazon.com company

First Edition

To Helen . . . my wife, my love, my best friend.

Acknowledgments

To my wife, Helen. Thank you for your love and unshakable commitment to our marriage through the arduous process of learning the keys outlined in this book. You're a rock of strength and a healing salve. You're truly my greatest gift.

To my dear friend, Richard Rich. Your friendship, encouragement, and accountability have helped me to become the man I am today. I'm truly grateful for you and your family for loving and supporting me and my family.

To my children—Luke, Lenea, Ginez, Christopher, and Gustavo. Thank you for your love and support, and for never giving up on me.

To Ann Castro, my developmental editor and Judaic/creative consultant. Thank you for the support and encouragement through this whole process. Thank you for challenging me to dig deeper.

To the AnnCastro Studio team who joined Ann on various phases of my book project—Jae Gravley (copyedit-proof phase and the graphic production artist who helped polish my design for the book's front/back cover) and Katrina Ann Martin (editorial-review phase). I appreciate your professionalism and attention to detail.

Contents

INTRODUCTION
Preparing for the Race

I've had the honor and privilege of walking with the Lord since I was a child. Now in my 50s, I can look back over a life filled with testimonies of the Lord's kindness and faithfulness, as well as countless opportunities to partner with the Holy Spirit, touching the lives of people at home and abroad.

I've served in various roles as a minister of the Gospel of Christ—youth pastor, associate pastor, pastor of new believers, men's pastor, and senior pastor. And I've ministered nationally and internationally, traveling to many places and connecting with individuals, churches, ministries, groups, and organizations in the body of Jesus Christ for various lengths of times and seasons.

In the spring of 2011, the Lord spoke a word to my heart, saying He was going to strip me of religion, traditions of men, and doctrines of demons. Of course, my inclination was to dismiss the word and rebuke the spirit that said it. After all, I'd been in ministry for over 30 years—evangelizing, making disciples, counseling, teaching, and preaching.

The ensuing months proved I'd heard the Lord's voice, which was beginning to juxtapose my thoughts, ideas, and beliefs with the simplicity of His written Word. The transition was both painful and liberating, challenging and empowering.

It also was something else—a spiritual shifting that closely paralleled truths I'd realized in my physical fitness journey.

As I crested the half-century mark, it had become quite clear that I needed to cut certain things from my life and diet, as well as develop—and maintain—a more solid, healthier bodily core for strength, balance, and injury prevention. A strong core would empower my body to work more cohesively, increasing effectiveness, coordination, and overall health.

It's no different for my spirit man—or yours. To get ready to run the race looming on the horizon, you and I must use this time to establish the basics and shore up any weakness in our spiritual foundation.

Any sports team that finds itself in trouble will tell you the first step to getting back on track is returning to the basics.

And that's exactly where every member of the body of Christ must go. In order to prepare for what's to come, it's imperative you and I take a step back—at least temporarily—from the creative solutions, processes, and patterns we adopted in this current age and visit the age-old foundations of our faith. They are the eternal, timeless, and changeless truths upon which everything is built.

We must reclaim our core. That means developing, boosting, and maintaining our spiritual health with the proper core truths and revelations based on the Word of God, ensuring the highest results, balance, and protection.

From a physical standpoint, my body is mature and, therefore, easily maneuvers in the patterns I've established. But there was a problem. For too many years, those patterns weren't keeping me in shape. Traveling from city to city and spending hour after hour in meetings, at the computer, eating at restaurants, and having inconsistent encounters with exercise were producing an increasing waistline and weakened muscles. Not to mention that my less-than-optimal health was increasing my chances of permanent damage, sickness, and disease.

Acutely aware I wasn't getting any younger—and realizing that any effort to get back into shape would be more difficult the longer I waited—a decision had to be made. I abandoned any excuses and began prioritizing my life. Due to my age and the challenges inherent with my physical condition, I had to acknowledge there weren't any quick fixes or shortcuts.

The same can be said of the church. She's been growing and developing for about 2,000 years—and isn't getting any younger. As a whole, the church has entered into a season of maturity, but some of the habits, thoughts, beliefs, and systems picked up along the way have increased her weight and decreased her health and overall effectiveness.

The world is precarious and filled with fear and uncertainty—within the church and without. Many believers are struggling to live in the peace promised to us and feel disconnected from the Lord, unable to find freedom from the entanglements of sin and the world. It's time we get into shape to prepare for the season we're living in. We must be deliberate as we reclaim the core of our life in Christ and restore the foundations of our faith. It's not the time for shortcuts or quick fixes. The transition from our once-comfortable patterns and processes will require purposeful, measured adjustments that are established in truth.

Quite frankly, the spiritual process the Lord has been taking me through has proven far more arduous than my physical fitness one. To my surprise—and shock, in some cases—some of the mainstream thoughts and ideas I've held on to proved to have little to do with the message of the gospel. In some cases, they were fruitless branches that looked nice, but produced nothing of lasting value. In other cases, they were poisonous impostors working against the very life flow of the Spirit.

Cutting away those branches was painful at first, but once I was free from the dead weight, I experienced more life pumping into those areas that were properly connected to the Vine. Areas of my life that had previously been frustratingly stagnant and troublesome were now filled with the victory I'd been promised. My life experience and relationship with the Lord was increasingly more congruent with what the scripture states is available.

Throughout this book, I've suggested certain topics be examined. That's not for the sake of argument or criticism, but analysis, and perhaps, a new perspective. I've no desire to second-guess, criticize, or condemn how we have done things in the past. Instead, let's consider that we stand on the threshold of a new season—one that, at the least, requires progression, and perchance, even a revolution.

There will be pain. Getting back into shape requires using muscles that haven't been used much. When my wife and I began to take our physical health to the next level, there was a lot of whining, complaining, and tears. From my wife too.

One of the biggest challenges was in our thinking—our thoughts clashing between what we could and couldn't accomplish. Sure, the strain on our muscles was difficult at times, but the greatest hurdles were thoughts of wanting to quit and doubting the process.

We learned our bodies were capable of going much further than our thoughts wanted them to go.

Likewise, developing new capabilities spiritually means pushing into areas beyond your current capacities. It requires pushing beyond the resistance of your current beliefs that try to convince you that you're less than who God says you are. You'll need to push beyond the limitations of thoughts, ideas, teachings, and doctrines that have restricted you from experiencing the fullness of life, love, joy, and peace available in Christ.

The universal cry I've heard among believers wherever I've traveled or ministered is that many of the structures, patterns, and processes we've been adhering to as a people and as ministers of the gospel, quite frankly, just aren't working. I'm reminded of the account in the Gospel of John where the disciples had labored through the night with barely anything to show for it. It seems we too have labored through times of darkness, but aren't seeing a return proportionate to our effort. Neither is what we're experiencing consistent with what the Lord has told us to expect.

Just as the day broke after the fruitless night and the Lord Himself commanded the disciples to press into the deep and put down their nets once again, so too I hear the same rumblings in my spirit. You and I must go beyond where we've been—and prepare for the harvest.

In this book, I've endeavored to focus primarily on reclaiming the core of our faith. In reality, that process must include unlearning things we've accumulated along the way. That's why I've intermittently addressed some opposing concepts—hoping you'll examine the questions, pruning shears in hand. As I submitted myself to the same challenge over the years, I've found many thoughts that I'd become familiar with were built on nothing more than rote tradition.

Accepting the challenge to examine the veracity of my beliefs against the Word of God has resulted in a recalibration of my faith. So if something I've written in this book challenges something you've held on to, I encourage you to exercise due diligence with that conflict.

Here are a few strategies I used to address questions I had:

1. **No proof-texting.** The practice of jumping from one verse to another verse to prove a point does little to establish truth and has caused a lot of confusion regarding the gospel.

2. **Consider the audience being addressed in a specific book, letter, or passage.** Oftentimes, this one step will do a great deal to clarify the intent of a passage.

3. **Establish the context.** To clearly understand a statement, it's imperative to understand the context in which it was given. Some truths are able to stand alone, outside of a contextual setting—but only after verifying the context. To bring certain truths from the Word in focus, I've added key passages of scripture, using the NASB translation. You'll notice I've included periodic glossary segments, information taken from *Strong's Exhaustive Concordance of the Bible*. I encourage you to follow the same steps to verify that I've properly conveyed the message of the verse without divorcing it from the context in which it was written.

If you follow these practical steps and land on a different conclusion than I have, I rejoice that the question may have helped you to become established more firmly so you may become fully persuaded in your faith.

Lastly, before we jump in, I've found that some of the core truths of the gospel seem to be at odds with one another—at least, initially. I humbly ask you to press through some of the sections that have had a polarizing force in the body of Christ. The issues of repentance, faith, grace, and forgiveness—as well as other truths—are all connected, but they require adequately examining each building block before you can clearly see how they fit together. I've added blank pages after each chapter to help you log your journey.

The thoughts, ideas, and perhaps *issues* shared in this book are rooted in one desire: help, not harm. My deepest heart desire is to present the same truths the Lord has shared with me, along with clear, actionable steps to remove the fat and strengthen the heart of your relationship with the living God—so you can reclaim your core and restore the foundations of faith.

—ᴡᴡ—

CHAPTER 1

Counting the Cost

Your life is filled with a cost-benefit analysis—everything from what movies you watch to whether or not you purchase a house. It's natural to expect the depth of analysis to be proportionate to the impact of what you're considering. That's why the most important decisions warrant a clear understanding of both what will be gained and what it will cost.

Without comparison, the most important decision you'll ever make—if you haven't already—is what kind of relationship you'll have with the creator of the universe. That one decision will impact your eternity.

I believe one of the most tragic missteps of the modern-day church is the minimization of both the cost and benefits of a relationship with Jesus Christ. Too often we relegate the monumental decision of eternity to a tagline at the end of a sermon or teaching. Certainly, most believers would agree that every opportunity should be made for the lost to be found—but are we truly giving this the weight it deserves?

When I ask a fellow believer how someone can be saved, the common response goes something like this: "Admit you're a sinner and be sorry for your sins, believe that Jesus died for you, and ask Him to come into your heart and be the Lord of your life."

That approach has elements of the truth, but it's a far cry from what the Word of God actually describes. Significant focal points of our efforts to "get people saved" are actually non-biblical and are missing the key elements of clarification and cost. Oftentimes, the invitation is sincere, and the verbiage may even be correct—but only to those who understand the meaning of the words.

1

Salvation, sin, forgiveness, and making Jesus Lord of your life are profoundly meaningful—if you're educated in their meanings. However, in the ears of the lost, there is no frame of reference. If an invitation is made, it should only be given after we're sure the full offer has been presented. There's a term for that in the business world: full disclosure.

Think of it this way. When I purchased my first home, I was amazed at the stack of papers I needed to review, and subsequently, sign. I'd been an avid writer since my youth—but can tell you this was the first time I ever got writer's cramp from signing my name. Not only did my signature indicate I agreed to the contents of the contract, but that I adequately understood the content as well. It was a mind-numbing experience to review and sign that contract . . . and that was just for a house!

If we're willing to give that much attention to a mere 30-year commitment to something that one day will rot and fade to dust, then it makes sense we should give even more attention to decisions affecting eternity.

Reflecting on the consequences of the banks making home loans affordable, I see some relevant comparisons to consider regarding the importance of counting the cost.

During the first decade of this millennium, there were literally millions of families who jumped into the dream of home ownership. The sharp increase in the cost of housing combined with a decline in lending standards—with little or no up-front cost and minimal requirements to qualify—shifted a significant portion of the housing market onto the backs of those who had little or no experience to hold the weight.

Not surprisingly, when interest rates started going up and house values dropped, the housing market began to shake. Interest-only loans became unmanageable, and upside-down mortgages shattered any motivation people may have had to keep their newly acquired homes. As a result, many abandoned their homes. The ripple effect crossed the nation, making it more difficult to reignite our economic engines.

So how does that apply to restoring your core and reclaiming your spiritual foundation? In a similar fashion, there currently are a large number of individuals who are connected to congregations all around this country, but who have little invested in their spiritual homes. The "no up-front cost and minimal requirements" approach to our relationship with

God has all but eradicated the difference between those professing to be Christians and those who don't.

According to the Barna Group research on *Temptations and America's Favorite Sins*, there is little difference between Christians and non-Christians regarding the rate of divorce, viewing pornography, or living lives filled with worry and anxiety. Just as the housing industry has experienced an epidemic of bankruptcies, so too are many families and congregations struggling with a moral bankruptcy due to following the same worldly approach.

By taking a brief look at the example the Lord gave us and considering His instruction to His disciples, you'll see that becoming His follower was much more than an impulsive response to an anemic invitation.

And He was saying to them all, "If anyone wishes to come after Me, he must deny himself, and take up his cross daily and follow Me. For whoever wishes to save his life will lose it, but whoever loses his life for My sake, he is the one who will save it. For what is a man profited if he gains the whole world, and loses or forfeits himself?" —Luke 9:23-25

The call was to follow Him—and the price was high to any who would belong to Him. The cost was the life of the follower.

Luke 14:25-35 tells of one account where large crowds of people were following Jesus as He walked through the dusty streets on His way to Jerusalem.

He stopped mid-step, turned, and spoke.

"If anyone comes to Me and doesn't hate his own father and mother . . . " He paused and looked through the crowd connecting with their eyes. "And wife and children and brothers and sisters . . . yes, and even his own life, he cannot be My disciple."

Quick glances among the crowd accented murmuring comments of disbelief.

Jesus raised the volume of His voice to cut through the rumbling. "Whoever does not carry his own cross and come after Me cannot be My disciple."

The religious leaders grumbled. His followers looked confused. But Jesus continued to speak.

"For which one of you, when he wants to build a tower, does not first sit down and calculate the cost to see if he has enough to complete it?"

The people nodded in agreement, some faces showing displeasure at the obviously rhetorical question.

"Or what about a king who sets out to meet another king in battle? Doesn't he first sit down and consider whether he is strong enough with ten thousand men to encounter the one coming against him with twenty thousand?"

Jesus was quiet again and so was the crowd. After a few long moments, He said, "So then, none of you can be My disciple who does not give up all his own possessions."

The message is as obvious now as it was then—we must count the cost before we commit to being His disciple. But along with discussing the cost, we must also consider the benefit.

The life He offers is eternal. As a point of clarification, eternal life is not heaven, nor is it a destination.

Eternal life is just what it says, participation in a life that has no beginning or end.

If and when you step across the threshold from your old life into the life that exists in Christ Jesus, your involvement in eternal life begins at that moment. That life is filled with love, peace, and joy, providing in abundance all you need. It is magnificent beyond your or my ability to understand or explain.

In the following pages, I will endeavor to present an accurate accounting of what is available to you and the price that must be paid to walk in it.

To begin reclaiming your core, the first step is the foundation of our Christian faith—the foundation that every aspect of your relationship with the Lord is built upon: The Word of God.

—⟱—

Reclaiming Your Core Journal
Chapter 1 Thoughts, Questions & Insights

CHAPTER 2
The First Covenant

A complex series of muscles make up your body's core—with key muscles in the belly area and mid/lower back. The core is a movement stabilizer, isometric and dynamic, that transfers force from one body extremity to another. Functional movements are highly dependent on the core's three-dimensional depth.

Far more than just helping you look good at the beach, the core is used to stabilize the thorax and pelvis during dynamic movement. Most, if not all, full-body functional movement originates in the core. It greatly affects your posture and aligns your spine, ribs, and pelvis to resist force, whether static or dynamic.

So your body's core not only allows you to move, but to stand firm.

It's also an integral part of continence and provides internal pressure to expel substances (vomit, waste, carbon-laden air, etc.). Women use their core muscles during labor and delivery.

As you can see, these muscles have a profound impact on almost everything you do on a day-to-day basis. Yet in spite of its importance, your core is mostly unseen.

And so it is with the Law of God.

Throughout my life as a believer, I've read numerous books, listened to thousands of teachings and sermons, and been touched by an innumerable amount of thoughts and ideas regarding the Christian faith—from cliché comments and bumper stickers to Facebook posts. I've always had a passion and commitment to the Bible—yet, the Lord brought me through a process that helped me realize I had adopted many cultural concepts as truth, even though there was little or no biblical foundation to support them.

There have been numerous areas where my beliefs have been sifted. But one of the key areas the Lord addressed was in regard to His Law. Just hearing the word *law* brought an immediate correlation with a list of dos and don'ts. The truth is that the Law is a beautiful picture of the heart and message of the gospel, foreshadowing the coming of Jesus.

There's much debate—and I might add, confusion—surrounding the Law and its relevance in the life of the believer. Throughout this book, we'll look at the Law and consider what role it has played in Israel, the Early Church, and in the life of the believer. It's foundational to everything that follows.

To understand what was being communicated in references to the Law, we must consider the understanding of those who heard this message when it was spoken. Since the message of the gospel was to the Jew first and then the Gentile—and the common understanding of the day was in reference to the God of the Hebrews—we must understand the terminology from the Jewish perspective of that time period.

When the Law is referenced in the Bible, it speaks specifically of the narrative of commandments given to the people of Israel in the desert before they entered the Promised Land. These commandments are referred to as the *Law of Moses* or *The Law*.

According to the Talmud—redacted in late antiquity and a key component in rabbinic teaching and literature that reflects the oral and written Judaic law—there are 613 commandments in the Law of Moses. A highly regarded rabbinic teacher in the 12th century, Maimonides, classified the 613 that are found throughout Genesis, Exodus, Leviticus, Numbers, and Deuteronomy.

Per Judaic culture, broadly speaking—the Law refers to the first five books of the Bible, termed the Torah and regarded as *Chamishah Chumshei Torah* (five fifths of the Torah):

- **B'reishit (Genesis)**—In the beginning/In a beginning
- **Shemot (Exodus)**—Names

- **Vayikra (Leviticus)**—He called
- **B'midbar (Numbers)**—In the desert
- **Devarim (Deuteronomy)**—Words or "stuff"

God's Glossary
Torah (Strong's H8451): torah (tow-rah). A feminine noun meaning instruction, direction, law, Torah, the whole law. Originated from the verb yarah (ya-rah, Strong's H3384), often translated as to teach/to instruct or law.

Far from being a divine list of dos and don'ts, His Torah is a spiritual roadmap. It's a powerful source of instruction and teaching—a place where we find wisdom, insight, and direction for our lives.

It can be argued that there are three divisions within the Law of Moses:

The Moral Law—Ten Commandments. Exodus 20:1-17.

The Social/Civil Law—Ordinances/rulings (mishpatim). Exodus 21:1-23:13. Also reflected in Deuteronomy 21-31, Leviticus 19-25, and Numbers 18, 26, 36.

The Ceremonial Law—Regulations/statutes for sacrificial offerings/worship. Exodus 25:1-31:18, Leviticus.

Judaically, the remaining books of the Hebrew Bible—termed the *Old Testament* by Christians—are divided into two other groups:

- **Prophets** (Nevi'im)
- **Writings** (Ketuvim)

Collectively, the entire Hebrew Bible—Torah, Nevi'im, and Ketuvim—is called Tanakh (tah-**nack**), an acronym made from the first Hebrew letter of the three divisions: TaNaKh. Looking via the purview of those who lived during Jesus' time and that of the Early Church, we easily can contextualize what they understood when they heard or read references to the Law, which encompassed the Torah, Prophets, and Writings.

These Hebrew Bible components are good—and filled with life. The key to understanding these writings is in how you view the information. It's absolutely critical to see these things from the perspective of Christ, not the perspective of humanity.

I will go into more depth as we progress through the foundations of our faith, but let me just say this:

In order to find life in the Law, you must access it through the cross. If you try to apply it through your carnal nature, it will bring death.

—⋙—

The Old Testament and the New Testament

When we consider the word usage of the 17th century, we'll have a better understanding of this division that we call the *Old* and *New* Testaments. The Hebrew word translated as *testament* in the 1611 King James Bible also is accurately translated as *covenant*.

God's Glossary
Covenant (Strong's H1285): b'riyt (ber-eet). A feminine noun meaning covenant, treaty, alliance, agreement.

The connotation implied by *testament* would be more accurately understood in modern terms as *covenant* or *agreement*. The Torah was an outline of the first covenant with Israel. In Christ, believers are partakers of a new covenant that was ratified—made officially valid—by His blood. During the last Passover meal that Jesus shared with His disciples, He said this:

And in the same way, He took the cup after they had eaten, saying, "This cup which is poured out for you is the new covenant in My blood." —Luke 22:20

The narrative that surrounds the life, crucifixion, death, burial, and resurrection of Jesus Christ explains the message of this new covenant in Him—and is contained in these books and letters, comprising the New Testament (Covenant) with its 27 books:

- **Historical Books:** Matthew, Mark, Luke, John, Acts
- **Pauline Epistles** (letters written by the Apostle Paul): Romans, 1 Corinthians, 2 Corinthians, Galatians, Ephesians, Philippians, Colossians, 1 Thessalonians, 2 Thessalonians, 1 Timothy, 2 Timothy, Titus, Philemon
- **Non-Pauline Epistles** (letters written by other authors): Hebrews, James, 1 Peter, 2 Peter, 1 John, 2 John, 3 John, Jude, Revelation

In the historical books—commonly referred to as the Books of the Gospel—Jesus referred to and quoted from the Law of Moses and the writings of the Torah. A great example is in the Sermon on the Mount, found in Matthew, chapters 5-7.

Jesus makes it clear that His purpose was not to do away with the Law of Moses or the Prophets. From the perspective of those hearing these words, they knew He was referring to what we call the *Old Testament*.

"Do not think that I came to abolish the Law or the Prophets; I did not come to abolish, but to fulfill. For truly I say to you, until heaven and earth pass away, not the smallest stroke of a pen will pass from the Law until all is accomplished." —Matthew 5:17-18

Throughout the narrative of the Sermon on the Mount—as well as throughout the four gospels—we find that Jesus not only affirmed the commandments that were given to Moses, He also increased the righteous requirements by clarifying the intent of the Law. Standing on a boulder on the side of the mountain, Jesus said . . .

"You have heard that the ancients were told [the Law], 'You shall not commit murder' . . . But I say to you that everyone who is angry with his brother shall be guilty before the court and

whoever says to his brother 'You good-for-nothing,' shall be guilty before the supreme court; and whoever says, 'You fool,' shall be guilty enough to go into the fiery hell." —Matthew 5:21a, 22

The religious leaders glared at the teacher. They had all the control they needed by reducing the Law of God to a pile of dos and don'ts. Jesus reinforced what had been written and disclosed the intent of the Law and Prophets.

Without diminishing the standard of the Law in the slightest, Jesus exposed the heart of God's expectations by living the example of following everything the Father expected. He further clarified what the Law is all about by summarizing everything that Moses had delivered from the Lord. All of the moral and social laws are summed up by two commandments quoted from Deuteronomy 6:5 and Leviticus 19:18.

And He said to him, "You shall love the Lord your God with all your heart, and with all your soul, and with all your mind. This is the great and foremost commandment. The second is like it, you shall love your neighbor as yourself. On these two commandments depend the whole Law and the Prophets." —Matthew 22:37-40

The ceremonial laws—which included instructions on worship, sacrifices, the priesthood, and the tabernacle—were given to point us to Christ and bring understanding to who He is and what He came to accomplish. They were types and shadows fulfilled in Christ, as evident in the book of Hebrews' narrative.

All of the various aspects of the Law given through Moses were a pattern, pointing to something better that was to come. The rules, ordinances, instructions, and details of the temple, priesthood, sacrifices, and worship were all given to help us know and understand the fullness of Jesus Christ when His time had come. Through Christ, a new covenant was established regarding the Law.

For this is the covenant that I will make with the House of Israel after those days, says the Lord: I will put My laws into

their minds, and I will write them on their hearts. And I will be their God, and they shall be My people.

And they shall not teach everyone his fellow citizen, and everyone his brother, saying, "Know the Lord," for all will know Me, from the least to the greatest of them. For I will be merciful to their iniquities, and I will remember their sins no more. —Hebrews 8:10-12 (quoting Jeremiah 31:33-34)

Viewing the first covenant through Christ, we see how the moral law, social law, and ceremonial law reveal the structure and standards of heaven. We can't understand what Christ did or why He had to do it without the Law. Neither will we understand how we are to live and what our lives should look like as He lives through us. It's through the scriptures we come to know the Lord more clearly, for the Law and the prophets speak of Him.

As we work through the process of how you can restore your core and reclaim your spiritual foundation in Christ, we'll progress through a number of passages of scripture—because the Word of God is eternal and alone is the standard by which every statement must be measured.

All Scripture is inspired by God and profitable for teaching, for reproof, for correction, for training in righteousness; so that the man of God may be adequate, equipped for every good work. —2 Timothy 3:17

At the core of God's Word—from Genesis 1:1 all the way through Revelation 22:21—is the message of His love for us and His desire for loving, familial intimacy with His people. That is the foundation of our faith.

Just as your physical core connects and empowers you to live and move, so the Word of God lies hidden at the center of your identity and connects and stabilizes everything your spiritual man does. It's in Him that you live, move, and have your very being.

Through the scriptures, He extends the invitation to relationship as we align our thoughts and beliefs with the Word of God. That is where transformation begins—and where your spiritual *fitness* kicks into high gear.

—m—

Reclaiming Your Core Journal
Chapter 2 Thoughts, Questions & Insights

CHAPTER 3
The Big 180

To begin the process of reclaiming your core and getting into shape, there has to be a change. That change starts in your mind.

The starting point of the message of the gospel is a call to repentance.

Firstly, let me set your mind at ease. This subject has nothing to do with an old, wild-haired man with an angry face pointing a finger at you. Nor does it have anything to do with an ominous-looking street person holding up a sign while earthquakes and tsunamis destroy the world.

Early in my walk with the Lord, my understanding of what God expected of me was to do my best to be good. My view of repentance was to make a 180-degree change in my direction, stop doing bad, and start following the rules of the Bible.

As a young minister, I was bi-vocational, working in construction to support my family and working in ministry to fulfill my call. I'm not sure how it was in Jesus' day, but my modern-day experience working with construction workers presented an environmental vocabulary that wouldn't be welcomed in most religious circles. Since I was trying to "be good," I'd daily promise myself that I wasn't going to swear. My intentions were noble—but my experience continued to be inconsistent with my desire.

"Lord," I cried out. "I want to stop cursing!"

From the depths of my heart, I heard the response, "**Instead of focusing on what you want to stop doing, identify and focus on what you want to do.**"

That was a powerful key that would start me on a path of transformation. The issue was focus.

"Lord, I want to glorify You with my words. I purpose in my heart to set my mind on what I want to come out of my mouth and seek to declare words of praise, worship, and thanksgiving in all situations."

Over the next several weeks, I regularly found opportunities to express my thankfulness and His praise. Days turned into weeks. I started to realize it had been several weeks since I had a colorful outburst. It wasn't that the difficulties weren't there, it was just that I had fixed my mind on praise—and that is what came out of my mouth. I had exerted no effort toward not swearing. I simply had set my mind on the Spirit.

Herein lies a valuable truth that brings us back to the core of who we are in Him—our focus determines our destination.

Before we look at specific passages of scripture that address the process of repentance, let's get a clearer understanding of what the word means. The commonly accepted meaning of repentance is to turn from sin to faith in God. That's not entirely inaccurate. In fact, it's incomplete and can be misleading.

God's Glossary
Repentance (Strong's G3340): metanoéō (met-an-o-*eh*-o). Derived from *metá* (me-*tah*), meaning *denoting change of place or condition* and *noéō* (noy-*eh*-o), meaning *to exercise the mind, think, comprehend*. It literally means to change the mind. As a believer, repentance is changing your mind in such a way that it causes you to turn from sin to faith in Jesus Christ.

Biblical repentance is the process of coming into agreement with God's Word and combining it with faith. The fruit of repentance is a transformed life. Simply put, repentance is the act and process of addressing our thought patterns. As it pertains to our relationship with the Lord, it's the process of comparing our thoughts, ideas, and beliefs with those of the Lord—and in response, coming into agreement with His Word.

We agree that anything God calls *sin* is sin—and those things that He regards as *righteous*, we also regard as righteous. When we agree with His Word and combine it with faith, it will produce a change in our thoughts, which will in turn produce a change in our behavior.

What is the Kingdom of God?

The call to repentance is a heavenly invitation to walk in the fullness of God's kingdom here on this earth. The kingdom of God is at hand—or put another way—is within reach. A life that partakes of and enjoys the fullness of His kingdom is available through a **persistent lifestyle of repentance**.

The kingdom of God is the realm where God is the king and ruler. According to the Word, His kingdom is righteousness, peace, joy, wholeness, healing, fruitfulness, and true riches, to name a few. It's a place where all the promises of God are yes and amen. It's a realm that has been made available to us through our relationship with Jesus Christ. Once again let me clarify, this isn't a reference to heaven, although certainly heaven is a part of His kingdom.

—⁂—

Where does repentance fit into the gospel message?

As we look at the biblical record of the repentance message, we clearly can see that it's at the leading edge of the Gospel of Jesus Christ.

> **Now in those days John the Baptist came, preaching in the wilderness of Judea, saying, "Repent, for the kingdom of heaven is at hand." For this is the one referred to by Isaiah the prophet when he said, "The voice of one crying in the wilderness, 'Make ready the way of the Lord, make His paths straight!'"** —Matthew 3:1-3

> **John the Baptist appeared in the wilderness preaching a baptism of repentance for the forgiveness of sins.** —Mark 1:4

From the onset of the Lord's season, the herald was crying out the message to prepare hearts to receive the King of Kings—and that message was to repent. John the Baptist was announcing that it was time for them to change their mind about what they thought they knew about the Lord and come into agreement with what He had said about His kingdom.

Repentance as a part of the gospel message isn't a new concept—but there is a key, inseparable aspect of this message that hasn't received much airtime: This same repentance is the condition for receiving forgiveness. Let me put it another way. If you don't change your mind and bring yourself into agreement with the commandments of the Lord and His Word to the extent that it produces a transformation in your life, you won't be forgiven of your sins.

John the Baptist also made it clear that repentance must be followed by persistent fruitfulness and a relationship with God that has nothing to do with religion, heritage, or affiliation.

> **Therefore bear fruit in keeping with repentance; and do not suppose that you can say to yourselves, 'We have Abraham for our father'; for I say to you that from these stones God is able to raise up children to Abraham. The axe is already laid at the root of the trees; therefore every tree that does not bear good fruit is cut down and thrown into the fire. —Matthew 3:8-10**

What about Jesus, what did He have to say about repentance? In the gospels, the first recorded words at the beginning of His public ministry were about repentance.

> **From that time Jesus began to preach and say, "Repent, for the kingdom of heaven is at hand."—Matthew 4:17**

> **The time is fulfilled, and the kingdom of God is at hand; repent and believe in the gospel. —Mark 1:15**

At the core of Jesus' ministry was a redirection, moving the focus away from the letter of the Law to the heart and intent of the Law. His message consistently pushed away the mindset of legalism toward an understanding of relationship with the Father. The call to repentance—a change in the way His followers thought—not only began, but permeated His ministry. Even after His resurrection, Jesus declared to the disciples . . .

Thus it is written, that the Christ would suffer and rise again from the dead the third day, and that repentance for forgiveness of sins would be proclaimed in His name to all the nations, beginning from Jerusalem. —Luke 24:46-47

It is important that we consider this declaration within the context it was spoken. Much of the understanding of Jesus' ministry was hidden to the disciples until after they were filled with the Holy Spirit. In this passage, the Lord was explaining a foundational purpose in His coming. Changing the way we think is at the core of our forgiveness and the beginning of our relationship with Him. That is the message that was and is to be proclaimed.

—ɯ—

Repentance in the Early Church

On the day of Pentecost—forty days after Jesus' resurrection—a disruption broke out on the busy streets of Jerusalem. Thousands of people gathered around the strange sounds of 120 people shouting praise and worship to God in multiple languages simultaneously.

Some words were familiar. Some just sounded strange. But something was happening, and people were rushing in to see what it was.

"These men are drunk!" someone shouted from the crowd. Some grunted their agreement, while others stood silent in wonder.

"These people are not drunk as you might think, after all it's only nine in the morning. But this is what the prophet Joel spoke about these last days." The crowds fell silent as Peter continued to teach them from the scriptures, revealing the predetermined plan of God in Christ Jesus. Their eyes were opened to the importance of His death and resurrection—and the Father's call to His children through His Son.

"Therefore let all the house of Israel know for certain that God has made Him both Lord and Savior—this Jesus whom you crucified."

At Peter's words and this revelation, their hearts were broken and they cried out, "What must we do?"

> **And Peter said to them, "Repent, and each of you be baptized in the name of Jesus Christ for the forgiveness of your sins; and you will receive the gift of the Holy Spirit." — Acts 2:38**

Once again the clear message is that you and I must repent—and that repentance is a conditional prerequisite to forgiveness. It's incumbent upon us to clarify that there is no biblical support for the idea that our forgiveness comes from anything apart from repentance. The teaching of repentance is foundational to our walk with the Lord. Without that foundation, we won't be able to grow to maturity in the Lord, nor will we be able to reclaim the core of our faith.

> **Therefore leaving the elementary teaching about the Christ, let us press on to maturity, not laying again a foundation of repentance from dead works and of faith toward God, of instruction about washings and laying on of hands, and the resurrection of the dead and eternal judgment. —Hebrews 6:1-2**

As the Apostle Paul spoke to the people of Athens, he referred to the time when God will judge the world. It extends beyond the bounds of the contemporary teachings throughout the ages and stands as the final punctuation—the end of the world as we know it. Until that day, the message is the same. All people everywhere should repent.

> **Therefore having overlooked the times of ignorance, God is now declaring to men that all people everywhere should repent, because He has fixed a day in which He will judge the world in righteousness through a Man whom He has appointed, having furnished proof to all men by raising Him from the dead. —Acts 17:30-31**

Any thorough and honest teaching regarding the good news of Jesus Christ must include the message of repentance. It's a core part of the New Testament's biblical narrative, from Matthew to Revelation. The message and meaning of repentance and what it entails are the keys that unlock the door to His kingdom and the practical application of God's Word in our lives. It's as vital to our spiritual health as changing our eating habits is to reclaiming our physical health.

—

Heaven rejoices

Jesus told a parable that demonstrated the heart of a shepherd—a willingness to leave the 99 in his flock that were safe and secure to find the one that was lost. When he found the lost sheep, he carried it back home, and then invited his friends and neighbors to rejoice with him. Jesus said this to the crowd:

I tell you that in the same way, there will be more joy in heaven over one sinner who repents than over ninety-nine righteous persons who need no repentance. —Luke 15:7

It should be stated that there's no indication of celebrating an event where a person silently raised her/his hand to accept Christ in a secrecy generated by a pastoral command that "everyone close their eyes, bow their heads, and refrain from looking around." Neither is there an indication where that person echoed a pastor's prayer, which also was echoed by everyone else in attendance so the person wasn't caused discomfort.

No, in fact the joy in heaven is specifically over a sinner who repents.

In the context of the culture Jesus was speaking to, the picture painted by the parable of the lost sheep depicted a sheep being removed from the wilderness through close fellowship with the shepherd. The sheep would spend most of the return trip resting on the shoulders of the shepherd— its ear near its owner's mouth, learning the sound of the shepherd's voice. The rescue would be complete when the sheep was restored to fellowship with the rest of the flock.

When those things happen in the life of a sinner, then there will be joy. Then the celebration will break out. Because repentance involves a change in thinking to agree with God, we find that confession is directly entwined with it.

God's Glossary
Confess (Strong's G1843): Exomologeō (ex-o-mo-lo-*gay*-o). From ek (Strong's G1537), meaning *out*, and homologeō (ho-mo-lo-*gay*-o, Strong's G3670), meaning *to assent*. Also means *to confess, admit, profess, or express agreement with*. Confession to God involves verbally and outwardly concurring with Him in His verdict.

Confession is the verbalization of a heart agreement. There was a point in my walk with the Lord where I had the revelation that it wasn't just the *sin of the world* that put Jesus on the cross—it was my sin. The penalty and punishment for every wrong that I had done, was doing, or ever would do had fallen upon Him.

The direct correlation between my sin and His pain became real to me. From that point on, I was acutely aware that every decision to disregard the truth in my life added to the weight that my Lord had to carry. It was through that revelation that I understood in a deeper way what God meant when He called something in my life *sin*. It was through that revelation that I confessed my sin, expressing my agreement that what He called sin, I also called sin.

When we truly begin to understand God's definition of sin and how our sin is responsible for the wrath that was poured out on our Lord, it's a natural response to acknowledge our agreement before Him and others. That was also the response of those who received the message of repentance from John the Baptist.

John the Baptist appeared in the wilderness preaching a baptism of repentance for the forgiveness of sins. And all the country of Judea was going out to him, and all the people of Jerusalem; and they were being baptized by him in the Jordan River, confessing their sins. —Mark 1:4-5

Along with the verbal agreement with the Lord regarding our sin, it's also appropriate to see our agreement displayed through our actions.

Many also of those who had believed kept coming, confessing and disclosing their practices. And many of those who practiced magic brought their books together and began burning them in the sight of everyone; and they counted up the price of them and found it fifty thousand pieces of silver. —Acts 19:18-19

Since the core of repentance is a change in our thoughts and beliefs, the process in our lives will have an effect both on our words and behavior. If our words and actions aren't affected or consistent with what we profess to believe, then we haven't truly embraced repentance.

Think of it this way. Your body is greatly impacted by the type and quantities of food you eat. If you fill yourself with processed food, candy, and other junk food, it will have a negative effect on your overall health. Likewise, the types of information you feed your mind impacts your spiritual man.

To reclaim your core and establish your foundation, you must replace your current thoughts and ideas with the truth.

Understanding what repentance truly represents is at the core of establishing the foundations of our faith. Later in the book, you'll learn the practical aspects of how to apply the principles of repentance. But first—since there's an excessive amount of misinformation regarding the subject—it behooves us to spend a little time discussing what repentance **is not**.

Reclaiming Your Core Journal
Chapter 3 Thoughts, Questions & Insights

CHAPTER 4
This Isn't That

You might truly desire to be healthy and in good physical condition, but without a change in your diet, you'll most likely continue to have the same result you've had up to this point.

The message Jesus came to deliver is that there is good news about your relationship with God the Father. He has a plan and a purpose for your life—and it includes love, joy, peace, and fullness in this life and in the next.

In order to partake of the life available to you through Christ, you will need to change the way you think. According to the biblical meaning and usage of the word for repentance, it's synonymous with *renewing the mind*.

In my walk with the Lord, the process of renewing my mind forced me to confront systems of thought that were in conflict with the truth in God's Word.

The sinful thoughts and beliefs I had held on to resulted in behavior that consistently fell outside of God's best for me. As I observed the fruit of those beliefs in my life, I realized I needed to root out anything robbing me of the abundant life, which is mine through Christ. The Holy Spirit—with my cooperation—began to convict me in areas of my life that weren't in agreement with His best for me.

At a young age, I learned to turn to alcohol for comfort. After a difficult day, a familiar thought would often visit me with the suggestion, "You need a drink."

I'm sure you can imagine that this belief led me into situations and circumstances that weren't healthy for my family or me.

It was through the process of seeking the Lord and hiding His Word in my heart that I learned an amazing truth: God is my comfort. Realizing I was looking to something other than my Lord to find comfort, I was confronted with a choice. I had created an idol of alcohol. I was at the point where I needed to choose—continue to use alcohol for comfort or believe what God had said in His Word about His being my comfort.

When you engage in this renewing-your-mind process, you'll find that repentance actually becomes a regular part of a spirit-led lifestyle. Coming to a clear understanding regarding what repentance is will be a huge part of growing in faith. But it's equally important that we tease out some misconceptions and identify what it isn't.

—⟋⟍—

Repentance is not . . . feeling bad, guilty, or sorry

However, it may include sorrow, regret and/or remorse for our sin. As a result of misunderstanding what repentance is, there are many people who associate a repentant heart with self-abasement, shame, and false humility. I've met many people who make a profession of faith, yet live in a constant state of shame and self-condemnation, believing they are exhibiting repentance.

In reality, that mentality is a total affront to the redemption freely given to us by the Lord, who took all of our sin and shame upon Himself so we could be free from it. To carry a perpetual awareness of our sin is to deny the righteousness imputed to us.

Although I may have a profound sense of sorrow or remorse when the Spirit points to an area of my life that isn't pleasing to Him, the emotion in and of itself has no value unless it gives me a nudge toward aligning my thoughts with the Lord's thoughts. Equally important is realizing that neither sorrow nor remorse for my sin is required. I can be living in a carnal pattern of thought resulting in sinful, destructive behavior, have the Spirit reveal it to me, and subsequently, change my mind to agree with Him— without feeling an ounce of regret.

—⟶

Repentance is not . . . works

There is a fatal error being taught in the body of Christ stating that repentance can't be a requirement for forgiveness because it would suggest we must work for—or in other words, do something to deserve—forgiveness.

That error is rooted in a misunderstanding of the word translated as *repent*. Since the popular meaning of repent is focused on our efforts to stop sinning and start doing good works, it seems to be a contradiction to what we know to be true—we're saved by grace through faith. However, when we understand that **repentance is about what we believe and not what we do**, we see that it's consistent with the testimony of the Word: It's our belief that results in forgiveness.

In order to be forgiven and declared righteous, we must acknowledge the truth about Jesus Christ and what was accomplished by His death and resurrection—and combine that knowledge with faith. Combining truth with faith is called belief. What we believe determines how we live.

> **And He ordered us to preach to the people, and solemnly to testify that this is the One who has been appointed by God as Judge of the living and the dead. Of Him all the prophets bear witness that through His name everyone who believes in Him receives forgiveness of sins. —Acts 10:42-43**

The Word is clear. We're not saved by works, but by grace through faith in Jesus Christ (Ephesians 2:8-9). True righteousness isn't about what we do as much as it is about who we are. Let me put it this way: If you're a good tree, you will produce good fruit. A bad tree can try as much as it wants to be a good tree, but it will never produce anything that isn't an outward expression of its own nature. If you're in Christ, you are a good tree because you've become one with Him, who is the good tree.

—〰—

Repentance is not . . . behavior modification

One of the great tragedies of our time is the focus on religious behavior modification instead of the transformation of heart and mind the Lord has made available to us through His sacrifice.

We must understand that simply changing our behavior will do nothing to bring us into the fullness of God's plans and purposes for our lives.

Behavior modification is nothing more than a dead form of religion that denies God's kingdom power. If the issue were simply behavior, then Paul wouldn't have considered all of his *good* deeds as rubbish (Philippians 3:8).

The goal must not be to change your behavior. Instead turn your focus to changing your mind to agree with God's Word.

When you agree with God's Word and combine that agreement with belief, it will produce a change in your heart that will affect your behavior.

You will walk by faith in Jesus Christ, which will cause you to turn away from sin, self-righteousness, and dead works. Faith comes by hearing. Filling your mind with the words of Christ develops your hearing (Romans 10:17).

As a result of misunderstanding repentance and what it is, many have become trapped in a cycle of self-righteousness, trying to change their behavior and growing increasingly disappointed and discouraged in the process. That never-ending cycle does nothing to destroy the root of destructive behaviors. And its related religious mentality drives people until they are exhausted, or even worse, become convinced they've attained righteousness by their own efforts.

When I'm getting ready for my workout, I can spend a lot of time and effort trying to deal with the issues in my life that try to keep me from working out. Or, I can just do my workout.

There are times in our lives where we must expend effort toward unraveling destructive thought patterns and processes, but the vast majority of struggles we face can be avoided altogether by simply changing our thoughts to agree with the truth that is in God's Word.

So if you're living by the grace that saved you, there will be outward evidence of that focus. Your behavior will change—not by your effort—but as a byproduct of your closeness to the Lord.

—m—

Repentance is not . . . optional

Repentance is required and can't be divorced from the message of the gospel. Too often we hear messages based on snippets of scripture, butchered from the context in which they were written. May the Lord's swift retribution fall on any of us who are picking and choosing statements and fragments from the Word that support any message contrary to His whole counsel.

I offer two warnings. The first is to those teaching any message that ignores passages of scripture that are in conflict with what you're trying to propagate.

If you continue to place these stumbling blocks before the Bride, you must prepare to fall under the hand of the Lord.

May I suggest that if you're not able to reconcile why there are two statements that seem to give a different message, you must seek the Lord for clarity before you teach a partial message to others. As a teacher, you will be judged more severely than others. You have a short time to repent.

The second warning I give is to everyone.

You have God's Word within your reach and the Holy Spirit—if you belong to the Lord. You're accountable to your shepherd to challenge the veracity of what men may teach, including the thoughts I present to you here.

There is only one shepherd—Jesus Christ the Messiah. You aren't dependent on any other human being to teach you, for the Holy Spirit will teach you all things. You are responsible to use what you've been given—which is everything you need for life and godliness—to be sure what you believe is in full agreement with Him and the sum total of His Word.

The renewal of your mind is at the core of a beautiful, lifelong engagement with the Creator of your soul. It's a progressive walk of freedom from sin and worldliness into increased fruitfulness and fulfillment of your destiny in Christ. It's a moment-by-moment walk in fellowship with the One who loves you and lives in you. There is no greater pursuit in this world than coming to know the Father and the One whom He has sent.

As you're transformed, you'll walk in an atmosphere that releases the very kingdom of God in and through you. It's a kingdom of life, joy, peace, and love.

Connected with repentance is the act of baptism—a demonstrative action expressing agreement with and adherence to the process commanded to enter His kingdom. This baptism into His death holds critical insight into understanding both the purpose and requirement of repentance.

—ɷ—

Reclaiming Your Core Journal
Chapter 4 Thoughts, Questions & Insights

CHAPTER 5

The Great Exchange: Part 1

rucified with Christ.

As the Lord walked me through the repentance process, it truly became a work of reclamation. A reclaiming of the core of who I am in Him and who He is in me. The work had to start with the foundation—the very building blocks of faith.

Reclaiming my physical core required my understanding the basics of physiology, proper diet, and exercise. As I worked through educating myself in the basics of each key area, I began to apply those newfound insights in conjunction with one another. Such is the process of reclaiming your spiritual core.

Over the next several chapters, we will be walking through the foundational truths of our faith in Christ. The first one is baptism.

In order to truly understand what it means to die with Christ in baptism, we must understand why He had to die. To understand His death, we must understand what sin is and its consequence. The best way to do that is to go back to the beginning.

In the beginning, God created the heavens, the earth, and everything in them. Among all creation, Adam and Eve were unique. They were created in God's image, but also were created to be in fellowship with Him.

God and Adam enjoyed that fellowship in the Garden of Eden. Within that relationship, Adam and Eve had full freedom to enjoy all of creation and partake of any fruit that grew there—with one exception. That one restriction was the fruit from the Tree of the Knowledge of Good and Evil.

In Genesis 3, there is an account referred to as *the fall* in the Garden of Eden. Through the skill of deception, the serpent began to twist the pure and simple truth of God's instruction. He focused on Eve, appealing to the nature of her flesh and leading her through a path of reasoning that caused her to question God's motives. Adam stood by and watched as his counterpart ate of the fruit—then, following suit, he ate the fruit as well. Through their disobedient act, sin and death were released in the world.

In addition to releasing a curse on the earth, Adam's disobedience opened a generational floodgate of death—its repercussions passed down to humanity ever since. Bringing it down to a personal level, death has been at work in you from the day you were conceived, regardless of status or station.

Paul states in Romans 6:23 that the wages of sin is death. That means that any time you and I deviate from the perfect will and standard of God, death is empowered in our lives.

The effects of sin are progressively degenerative, but the righteous standard of a holy God will never diminish. No one can live a life that measures up to God's standards. Because of that, you and I have been contributing—knowingly or unknowingly—to the case for judgment against us.

Understanding the implications of sin begins by knowing what God means when He refers to sin and righteousness.

God's Glossary
Righteous (Strong's H6662): Tzaddik (*tsah*-deek). Adjective meaning *just* or *righteous*. It's the state of being right or justified righteousness. Conformity to God's standards of what is right, justifiable.

Sin (Strong's H2398): Chata (chah-*tah*). Verb meaning *to miss* or *to go wrong*. Missing the true end and scope of our lives. An offense in relation to God's righteous standards.

In reality, God's standard of righteousness is much higher than we're able to comprehend. Ask the average person *what is sin?* and the reply will fall along the lines of the Ten Commandments—murder, lying, stealing, adultery, etc. To be right with God involves much more than simply avoiding evil behavior.

As a young believer in my teenage years, I recall having the thought process that doing a good deed would justify any other bad behavior I may have engaged in throughout the day. My goal was to make sure I found at least one good thing to do each day to make up for the regular participation in the things I thought were wrong. Sadly, I've encountered many adults—even believers—who still hold to the idea that their good works will function as a counterweight to their sin.

There is a gross misunderstanding and underestimation regarding the weight and consequence of sin. Many have falsely supposed religion is an opposing weight to the burden of sin where our *good deeds* have the capacity to outweigh our *bad deeds*. This couldn't be further from the truth. The truth is that anything done outside of a living relationship with Jesus Christ that isn't in complete agreement with Him is sin. That even includes donating a million dollars to a charity.

According to God's definition, sin is not only violating His standards (laws), but failing to fulfill the purpose for which He created us. Both our *good* and *bad* deeds are stacked on the scales of justice against us—they are equally offensive to a holy God.

As shared, all humanity since the dawn of creation—with only one exception, which will be discussed shortly—has fallen dreadfully short of the expectations of the holy God who created us. Sin and death became our masters and have reigned over humanity, keeping us locked up in our guilty state with no hope of ever being able to be free. Clearly stated in Romans 3:23, all have sinned and fall short of God's approval.

So what hope do we have? Without exception, there is no hope in and of ourselves. The truth is, the story just goes from bad to worse, and now, to nightmare. But hang on, good news is coming.

The penalty for violating the standards of God's law and failing to fulfill His purpose for our lives is death. The only way you, I, or anyone can pay for sin is with a life. But not just any life, it must be the life of someone who has lived up to every expectation of God's standard of righteousness.

Enter hope. So you and I—along with all humanity—were totally lost, excluded from any promise or provision, having no hope and living without God in the world. But God loved us. He sent His Son to redeem us, to pay the price of death for our sins—literally, to purchase us. Since only a perfect offering would satisfy the debt, it had to be the blood of Jesus Christ, who was given as the sacrifice, or payment, for our sin.

To clarify: God does not forgive us because He loves us. His love for us caused Him to give His only begotten Son to shed His blood to pay the penalty and price for our sin, not to dismiss it.

It's only through faith and acceptance of the price paid for us that our sins can be forgiven.

Building on the foundational truths discussed in chapter 3 regarding repentance, faith is the next key aspect of reclaiming your core. You must believe in order to receive the benefits of the price Jesus Christ paid, namely forgiveness for our sins.

Remember that repentance means to change your mind—to agree with what God says in such a way that it produces fruit. Inseparable from repentance is faith. It's impossible to agree with something you don't even believe in. It's equally impossible to truly believe (biblically speaking) in something that has no effect on your behavior.

As a young man and new believer, I struggled deeply with my identity. When I would look at my reflection, all I could see was what I believed made me unlovable. I hated myself. I hated every blemish, every flaw, every feature I thought was less than attractive. I would stand in front of the mirror and tell the man I saw, "I hate your <expletive> guts!"

One day as I was expressing my disgust for the man in the mirror, I heard the Lord ask me a question.

"How can you say you love Me and hate what I've created?"

That question broke me and I wept. Never had I heard a rebuke so sweet, nor a word of correction so filled with hope and healing.

For the first time ever, when I looked into the mirror, I saw someone who was created with intention. I saw a young man, designed and fashioned on purpose. I wasn't a mistake, nor were my eyes, my mouth, my body, my hair, my nose. I was made by someone who loved me. I was made the way I was because that was how He wanted me to be—and He loved me just the way He made me.

From that day on I had a choice to make every time I looked in the mirror.

Would I agree with my fractured sense of myself or would I believe the One who created me and knew me better than I knew myself?

Would I agree with the world and the enemy of my soul or put my faith in the One who cannot lie?

Would I continue to hate what God said He loves or would I believe what He said was true and learn to love what He loves, including myself?

At the heart of this struggle in my life were the components of repentance, faith, and belief. I was confronted with a truth that was contrary to what I had believed about myself. I could have hardened my resolve to hold to the belief that I was as worthless as gum stuck to a shoe—or I could change my mind to agree with what I heard the Lord say to me.

I allowed myself to be persuaded by the truth and put my faith and agreement in the affirmation of God's love for me. From that day on I confronted any opposing thought with the substance of what the Lord had told me. My thoughts, and subsequently my behavior, changed.

God's Glossary
Faith (Strong's G4102): pistis (*pih*-stis). Feminine noun meaning *faith* as in *to win over, persuade*. Subjectively, meaning *firm persuasion, conviction, belief in the truth, veracity, reality.*

Believe (Strong's G4100): pisteuō (peh-*stu*-oh). The future tense is pisteusó (pist-*yoo*-o), from pistis (Strong's G4102). Meaning *to believe, have faith in, trust.*

The words *faith* and *believe* in God's Word carry the following connotation: To trust in, rely on, and adhere to. It's not simply giving a mental assent to information. Faith embodies the engagement and agreement of the heart, and resonates within the very core of who we are.

By our agreement with and trust in the provision of Jesus Christ's sacrificial death, we receive forgiveness for all of our sin and failures. There is absolutely nothing we could have done to be cleansed from the filthiness of our own sin, so God made a way for us through His Son. But there is still more we need to examine in this regard.

When Jesus Christ went to the cross, He didn't just take your sin—He took you.

Consider the clarity of Paul's wording in the following passages:

For the love of Christ controls us, having concluded this, that one died for all, therefore all died; and He died for all, so that they who live might no longer live for themselves, but for Him who died and rose again on their behalf. —2 Corinthians 5:14-15

I have been crucified with Christ; and it is no longer I who live, but Christ lives in me; and the life which I now live in the flesh I live by faith in the Son of God, who loved me and gave Himself up for me. —Galatians 2:20

For you have died and your life is hidden with Christ in God. —Colossians 3:3

It is a trustworthy statement: For if we died with Him, we will also live with Him. —2 Timothy 2:11

Each of these passages is filled with powerful keys for living the life of a follower of Jesus Christ. We'll revisit and unpack them in greater detail in subsequent chapters.

Before moving on to the truths about living a resurrected life, we must understand that without death, there is no resurrection. Identifying with Christ in the life made available to us through His resurrection means first identifying with Him—and joining Him—in His death. Death means separation from life. In this case, it's a willing separation from the life of sin, the world systems, and our own efforts to be righteous.

The importance of this first step can't be overstated. It's at the core of our mandate to count the cost. This decision requires placing everything at the cross—that includes our hopes, dreams, careers, relationships, sins, good deeds, addictions, possessions, and so on.

And in that moment, we acknowledge and agree that **anything the Lord wants to remove from our lives is destined for the grave** and **only what He chooses to bring to life can follow us into the life ahead**.

Practical footnote: There may be things that are part of your life now that you may not yet realize aren't part of God's plans and purposes for you. Not to worry. Those things will be part of the process that will follow and be discussed in upcoming chapters. The critical understanding we must have at the onset of our walk with the Lord is that this is a lifelong commitment.

We are agreeing He has the full right and freedom to require anything of us at any time for as long as we live. We literally are surrendering our life to His lordship and rule because we have been purchased with the price that He alone has paid.

By His grace, through faith and repentance, our life intersects with Jesus Christ at the cross in death. By the shedding of His blood, at that very moment, our sins were forgiven and we were justified and declared righteous.

God's Glossary

Justify (Strong's G1344): dikaióō (deh-ki-*ah*-o). Contracted dikaió, future is dikaiósō, from díkaios (Strong's G1342) and means *just, righteous, to justify*. In the New Testament, dikaióō in the active voice means *to recognize, to set forth as righteous, to declare righteous, to justify* as a judicial act.

In Him we have redemption through His blood, the forgiveness of our trespasses, according to the riches of His grace which He lavished on us. —Ephesians 1:7-8a

Therefore, having been justified by faith, we have peace with God through our Lord Jesus Christ, through whom also we have obtained our introduction by faith into this grace in which we stand; and we exult in hope of the glory of God. —Romans 5:1-2

Much more then, having now been justified by His blood, we shall be saved from the wrath of God through Him. —Romans 5:9

Through His death and resurrection, Jesus Christ reclaimed the innocence lost by Adam and Eve in the Garden of Eden. Your sins were forgiven and you were justified—that is, declared to be in right standing with God by His blood. The righteousness of Jesus Christ was given to you, and you were declared righteous in the courtroom of heaven. The fellowship that was lost now is regained and available in the One who gave His life to purchase it.

This truth is at the heart of reclaiming your core. Your core identity and the bedrock of your foundation is the reality that Jesus Christ has reclaimed all that was lost through the fall—and that you've already been made complete in Him.

Your association with the cross represents the end of everything that preceded it. But that death is merely the beginning point of a mystery that will unfold around you for the rest of your life. Without the cross and your participation with Christ on it, you won't have any participation in anything that follows.

As it is in the natural, the first thing that follows death is the grave. The grave is where you and I must go next as we move forward in the restoration of our own foundation.

—ɱ—

Reclaiming Your Core Journal
Chapter 5 Thoughts, Questions & Insights

CHAPTER 6

The Great Exchange:
Part 2

Buried with Christ.
The only proper destination for a dead body is the grave.

Peter said to them, "Repent, and each of you be baptized in the name of Jesus Christ for the forgiveness of your sins; and you will receive the gift of the Holy Spirit." —Acts 2:38

Baptism in the name of Jesus Christ is an actual part of the repentance process and can't be separated into a unique experience. Our acceptance of what Jesus Christ accomplished on the cross as payment for our sins inextricably joins us together with Him in His death and the burial of His earthly body.

To truly accept what's been done on our behalf is to recognize that there is nothing you or I have ever done, are doing, or ever will do that can measure up to God's standard of holiness. The only possible solution is that our lives outside of Jesus Christ cease to exist. Herein lies the significance and importance of baptism.

Within the body of Christ, there are some who hold to a school of thought that baptism is simply an outward expression of an inner experience. In reality, it's much more than that. It's a vital component in a spiritual transaction—one that you and I must partake in so the foundation of the gospel's pattern and plan can be restored.

This initial act of obedience represents both an understanding and agreement with the truth that you must be buried with Christ—by first dying to everything that existed outside of who God has created you to be. This step is a key aspect of participating in the kingdom of God.

At this point, I'm compelled to make a few comments. Firstly, I know there are some who have argued whether or not a believer needs to be baptized to be saved. May I submit, to argue that point is to miss it entirely. If you're of the position that you need to argue the need—you're not ready for what follows baptism.

My advice: Keep your clothes dry and wait until you understand the significance of what you have been commanded to do.

There were several things Jesus commanded His disciples to do as they began to walk in what He purchased through His death and resurrection:

Go therefore and make disciples of all the nations, baptizing them in the name of the Father and the Son and the Holy Spirit, teaching them to observe all that I commanded you. —Matthew 28:19-20a

They were instructed to make disciples (not converts), baptize, and teach all disciples to observe (keep, obey) all that He commanded them to do. Here is the point: To be a disciple is to live out a lifelong commitment to obey everything Jesus Christ commands you to do. The first step of that journey is death, which is portrayed through baptism.

As I've walked through the process of reclaiming the core of my faith, I've struggled through various aspects of the place and purpose of baptism. For example, there are other passages that address the process of being saved, but don't mention baptism or repentance. These scriptures state it's through faith—or calling on the name of the Lord, or believing—that we're born again. At first glance, it may seem, even as some have suggested, that the scripture is contradicting itself. As a result, there are some folks who use these passages as an argument to suggest that neither baptism nor repentance is required.

This is a great example of the danger of proof-texting. In my own journey, the folly of picking and choosing passages caused me a lot of confusion—and was one of the first areas the Lord focused on when He began stripping me of things that weren't built on a solid foundation.

We should never make the mistake of believing anything that requires us to disregard something that is explained elsewhere.

So if we were to carry that faulty logic forward, it would remove repentance, baptism, and obedience from the requirements of salvation because they aren't mentioned in other passages. And then we could argue that based on Acts 2:38, neither faith, grace, nor calling on the Lord are required to be saved since they aren't mentioned there.

Beloved, we are instructed that it is the *sum* of His Word that is truth.

There is no option for us to pick and choose the verses that support what we want to believe, nor to discard those that don't. We must look at all passages that discuss any given subject and see how the Holy Spirit has woven them together in truth.

Now, back to baptism.

Outside of understanding and identifying with the death of Christ, there is no life in Him. There is no promise, no hope, no redemption, and no salvation without being joined with our Savior in His death. There is no relationship with the Father, no rebirth, no sanctification, and no promise of eternal life outside of this truth.

What shall we say then? Are we to continue in sin so that grace may increase? May it never be! How shall we who died to sin still live in it? Or do you not know that all of us who have been baptized into Christ Jesus have been baptized into His death? Therefore we have been buried with Him through

baptism into death, so that as Christ was raised from the dead through the glory of the Father, so we too might walk in newness of life. For if we have become united with Him in the likeness of His death, certainly we shall also be in the likeness of His resurrection, knowing this, that our old self was crucified with Him, in order that our body of sin might be done away with, so that we would no longer be slaves to sin; for he who has died is freed from sin. — Romans 6:1-7

As we begin to look at what it means to be raised with Him, it will become increasingly clear that there is nothing of our old life that we can bring into our new life. The failure to clarify this truth has caused much confusion in the body of Christ. Some continue to live under the unbearable guilt and condemnation of past sins, and others busy themselves with efforts to be clothed in the vile and disgusting garments of self-righteousness. Others live in a godless form of religion that looks good on the outside, but provides no power to live in God's purposes or plans. These have no part in the kingdom of God, but you wouldn't know it by looking at them from the outside.

To truly embrace the wonderful mystery of our union with the death of Christ on the cross and our submersive baptism into the grave, we must have a glimpse of the joy awaiting us on the other side. We can face this end with great hope when we begin to realize what is ending and what is beginning.

You can be assured that what has ended can in no way compare to what follows any more than a sequoia redwood seed buried in the ground can compare to what grows from it.

Just as you have died and have been buried with Christ, so also have you been raised with Him in His resurrection. The great exchange included giving up your old life so you could gain His new life. The next step in the reclaiming-your-core process is understanding the life available to you now.

—⁓⁓—

Reclaiming Your Core Journal
Chapter 6 Thoughts, Questions & Insights

CHAPTER 7

The Great Exchange: Part 3

R aised with Christ—righteousness.
It's both the cross and the resurrection of Jesus Christ that are the focal point of the gospel.

In the previous chapter, we looked at Romans 6:1-7 as it relates to our death and burial with Christ. As we move forward to consider the resurrection, we must realize that just as it pertains to Christ Jesus, it also pertains to all of us who have been crucified and buried with Him.

> **Therefore we have been buried with Him through baptism into death, so that as Christ was raised from the dead through the glory of the Father, so we too might walk in newness of life. —Romans 6:4**

Prior to reclaiming my core, my walk with the Lord largely consisted of what I would call a *sin-conscious life*. The majority of my focus was trying to address the behavior that I felt was inconsistent with what the Lord expected of me. I existed in a tiresome cycle of trying to be good, failing, confessing my sin, and praying for the strength to do better. I had placed my hope on the removal of things I thought were keeping me from the resurrection life of Christ in me. But there was a problem. I'd been focusing on trying to make my old life better instead of walking in the resurrection life that was given to me.

The hope of the gospel is this: He is alive in us and we're alive in Him. We live for Him, through Him, and with Him. That hope is only possible if we've been crucified, buried, and raised with Him in the Spirit. Our focus must shift from what has died and been buried to the new life that's before us.

Our salvation isn't fulfilled through the payment of the penalty of our sin—it's by our identification with Christ and His life. The identification made possible by the cross.

Paul states quite clearly to the Corinthians as he is discussing the resurrection (per 1 Corinthians 15:13-19):

> **But if there is no resurrection of the dead, not even Christ has been raised; and if Christ has not been raised, then our preaching is vain, your faith also is vain. And if Christ has not been raised, your faith is worthless; you are still in your sins. —1 Corinthians 15:13-14, 17**

At this juncture in the reclaiming-your-core process, you need to step back slightly and examine where you are. **This is a point of convergence— where you must establish how these truths work together.**

Everything discussed throughout the remaining chapters focuses on living our lives in the resurrection life.

—ᴍ—

Waking up to a resurrected life

The various parts of our body may be studied and observed individually, but they must never be removed from their connection or context— otherwise, we will die. So too we must keep the core aspects of the gospel message connected to every subject we discuss.

Just like the muscles, heart, and lungs are critical to our body, so too are the truths about repentance, faith, the blood of Jesus Christ, the cross, baptism, and resurrection critical to our walk with the Lord.

Each aspect of the work of Jesus Christ is interdependent with the others. The resurrection without the cross would be impossible, just as the cross without the resurrection would be useless.

Watch how the heart of the gospel pumps the message of the blood of Jesus Christ through the core of our faith:

- It was by living a perfect life that Jesus fulfilled the Law and all righteousness as a man. That was required to establish authority over the world and to reclaim all that was relinquished by Adam through the fall. Jesus had to be fully righteous in order to be the perfect, spotless sacrifice to pay for our sins.
- He had to bear the punishment for our sin. It was His torture and death on the cross that satisfied the wrath of God for sin.
- His blood had to be poured out as that perfect sacrifice to pay the price for our sin. Without it, we would have no forgiveness and couldn't be justified or declared righteous.
- There needed to be a death and burial to end the rule of sin, death, and the flesh.
- And there had to be the resurrection to release His life to the vessels that had been made clean by His blood and set apart by His sacrifice. Without the resurrection life of Jesus Christ in us, there would be no life in us at all. Without His resurrection life, we have no power, ability, or authority to live in obedience to Him.

But God, being rich in mercy, because of His great love with which He loved us, even when we were dead in our transgressions, made us alive together with Christ (by grace you have been saved) and raised us up with Him, and seated us with Him in the heavenly places in Christ Jesus. —Ephesians 2:4-6

Jesus Christ is the way. He is the truth. He is the life. There is no way to come to the Father except through Him. His power is directed toward us and brought about in Christ through the resurrection. It's in this resurrected life that we live—and only in His life that we can live.

At this point of convergence, we must break away from the idea that our ability to enter into or maintain a relationship with God has anything to do with our own righteousness or ability. The price that had to be paid for our sin has been paid. Our life of sin and self-righteousness—including the good and bad we have done—is gone. It has been crucified with Christ and is dead and buried in the grave of baptism. The life we live now is in Him—for it is in Him that we live and move and have our being.

Blessed be the God and Father of our Lord Jesus Christ, who according to His great mercy has caused us to be born again to a living hope through the resurrection of Jesus Christ from the dead. —1 Peter 1:3

. . . and He Himself bore our sins in His body on the cross, so that we might die to sin and live to righteousness; for by His wounds you were healed. —1 Peter 2:24

He raised us with Him so we could live out the rest of our lives by His indwelling Spirit. The following chapters reveal what that looks like and the process we need to engage in. But before we move to the practical aspects of a life lived in Christ, we must have a solid understanding of the core truths of the cross, the grave, and the resurrection.

I lived much of my early life trying to be a good Christian be-fore realizing I was trying to be something I already was.

The great and mysterious truth is that when we are born again, we are literally born anew from above.

Even in the beginning stages of my walk—after I received the revelation that I was already beyond what I was striving for—the proverbial lightbulb started to go off. My perception of myself and the world around me began to dramatically change. It was the first major breakthrough in reclaiming the core of who I already am.

The Lord opened my eyes to see the spiritual realm as He pointed to how life functions in the natural. Consider how a child is born. It does nothing to deserve or attain the life it receives. It has but to breathe. So it is in the Spirit. Our new man is birthed in the womb of our faith when the seed of the Word is received in our heart. Once that birth takes place, there is no need to try to be anything—we already are what we will be. The process is one of discovery.

It's the great exchange—something taken, something given. That's what happened when you came to Christ. Your old life, the curse of sin, and a life of separation were removed. In exchange, you received a new life . . . a life from God, not of this world. You were born anew from above and are literally part of something that hadn't existed on this planet prior to Christ.

> **For the love of Christ controls us, having concluded this, that one died for all, therefore all died; and He died for all, so that they who live might no longer live for themselves, but for Him who died and rose again on their behalf. Therefore from now on we recognize no one according to the flesh; even though we have known Christ according to the flesh, yet now we know Him in this way no longer. Therefore if anyone is in Christ, he is a new creature; the old things passed away; behold, new things have come. —2 Corinthians 5:14-17**

From the moment you are born anew from above, you are something, or should I say, someone, who has been made into something new. You aren't what you were before—and you will never be that again.

This truth is a critical foundation that will help to support what will be built in your life as you reclaim your core. In fact, the revelation of who you are in the resurrected life of Christ is the core. If you don't understand who you are, the process of maturity will be confusing.

When I began my fitness journey, I was more than 40 pounds overweight. I started to consistently exercise my muscles, but it only took several weeks to feel the effects. I was able to do more exercise for longer periods of time before hitting my maximum heart rate. I knew my muscles were getting more toned and stronger, even though you couldn't tell by looking at my outer appearance. I was convinced that I had an awesome set of six-pack abs—hidden beneath a cushion of fat.

If I consistently apply the fitness principles that transformed my muscles, then I'll continue to diminish the layer of fat that distorts my physical definition.

In some ways, our spiritual journey is the same. We've been changed inside. Through the consistent application of identifying with our true self, we can lose the part of our nature that distorts the image of who we truly are in the Lord.

Many believers, including the Apostle Paul, have grown frustrated at times with the experiential realities of living as a new creation—when our behavior continues to be inconsistent with the realities of who we have been created to be in Christ. To reclaim our core and establish a solid foundation, we must address this inconsistency head on.

Reclaiming Your Core Journal
Chapter 7 Thoughts, Questions & Insights

CHAPTER 8
Truth vs. Experience

A ddressing the disparity between the truth and our experience. Everything covered up to this point has been to lay the foundation for what comes next: application.

When I first began applying the principles of health and fitness as a mid-life, overweight, under-athletic man, my body revolted. My stomach hated my dietary decisions (less ice cream, more salads). My heart and lungs screamed at me during workouts. My muscles punished me for days each time I pushed them beyond their limits. My comfortable human experience was completely turned upside down.

Sure, I had learned that fitness, nutrition, and exercise were an important part of reclaiming my physical core. But without the proper information, I could have ended up doing more damage than good—expending a lot of effort without achieving the results. You can know everything there is to know about health and fitness without attaining a single benefit. In order to achieve your fitness goals, you have to apply what you've learned.

Within that context, there are two vital ingredients to success. The first is knowing the right information. The second is applying it. I realize this is obvious—and trust me when I tell you, I am in no way attempting to be condescending. Instead, I'd like to highlight the reality that even though I have the right information, my body isn't as quick to get on board with my fitness program. Therein lies the problem.

Once again, that example works for our spiritual life. Our spiritual walk needs to go through an upheaval. It won't be pleasant. There was a pseudo-comfort we enjoyed while we were uninformed. Although weighed down, unsatisfied, and weary, we were familiar with our world. But as we learn the truth of the gospel and the cost to enter His kingdom, a crisis will arise. It's the clash of how our life looks compared to the vast riches of Christ and His kingdom, as defined by the scriptures—fullness of joy, unshakeable peace, and a life that reflects the righteousness of the resurrection life of Christ in us.

Paul—in Romans, chapter 7—succinctly captures our struggle and, with artisan skill, displays the core of our conflict:

For I know that nothing good dwells in me, that is, in my flesh; for the willing is present in me, but the doing of the good is not. For the good that I want, I do not do, but I practice the very evil that I do not want. —Romans 7:18-19

In my natural body, the willing was present, but the doing wasn't. I wanted to be healthy. But the more I learned about what I should and shouldn't eat, the more frustrating it was. It became increasingly difficult to enjoy a nice bowl of ice cream before I went to bed.

The more I learned and attempted to do the exercise and activity required to whip my muscles into shape, the more I realized that I had much farther to go than I had hoped. I had the right information on how to be healthy, but I struggled in the application.

Knowing the right things to do caused a conflict in me. This crisis continued to increase as I walked in ways that were detrimental to my health and well-being.

So too spiritually, this crisis must come.

There's a point when we need to make a choice. Will I continue in patterns of self-destruction—which often lead to burdens of guilt and shame—or will I begin to apply what I know?

I would like to call attention to a specific phrase that's key to our growth: begin to apply.

When I decided to apply effort toward my knowledge of exercise and fitness, I can assure you it wasn't pretty. At the beginning of my fitness revival, I had set a goal to do a 5K run before my 50th birthday. My initial attempts at fitness involved walking/jogging on a treadmill, along with some dietary modifications.

Running five kilometers (without the walking intervals) seemed like a noble and attainable goal. And yet, one month before my 50th birthday, I still hadn't made it the full 3.1 miles. (I don't know about you, but I prefer the sound of 5K to its equivalent 3.1 miles—it just sounds further.)

Three weeks before my deadline, I decided I was going to go for it. I set the speed on the treadmill and started on my quest.

The first mile wasn't bad—I had already breached that milestone multiple times.

The second mile came with increased heart rate and breathing.

The third mile . . . changed things. It seemed like things were leveling off, although my legs felt a little rubbery.

The final tenths of miles—and yes, I counted every one—were exciting. That's when I realized I was going to achieve my first major fitness goal. I wrapped up my 5K at about 33 minutes and went into my cool-down feeling like an Olympian (that is, in the Olympics of middle-aged, out-of-shape, overweight people).

I walked out of my session and got my heart rate and breathing back to normal—then noticed my legs had gone from rubbery to wobbly. My muscles were making it quite clear that they weren't happy. For the next three or four days, they reminded me of their displeasure again and again.

Even though it was hard and even though the recuperation was painful, I found great encouragement in the fact that I had begun to apply what I had learned—and was making progress.

Our walk with the Lord is a growth process. It's the cultivation of a living relationship with the person of Jesus Christ through the power of the Holy Spirit. It must be clearly understood that the application in the natural of what has already taken place in our spirit is applied in our day-to-day lives as a process that develops over time.

As I began to understand the truth regarding who I am, my focus began to shift from my behavior that was outside of God's best for me to what He was doing in and through me in the moment. I had spent so much time trying to stop my sinful flesh that I was almost oblivious to the amazing things the Lord was doing in me. I had gone from one problem to the next, living from defeat to defeat.

But when my eyes were opened to the reality of what had already been done, I began to see the progress in my walk with the Lord. I went from victory to victory.

I remember when the Lord asked me a question that brought a fresh clarity regarding His heart on the matter of growth.

"Son, when your child took his first two steps and fell, did you spank him for falling?"

"Of course not," I said.

"Then why would you think I am disappointed in you when you fall? Just like you celebrate the progress of your child, so I delight in yours."

May you find great comfort in knowing that God is okay with the process you are—and will be—going through. His grace, mercy, and love are more than enough to both empower you to grow and to complete the work He began in you.

You'll need that comfort as you navigate the frustration of reconciling your experience with the reality of who you are. Your inner man is in complete agreement with the Lord—but there is a process to your outer man living in a manner that is congruent with the truth. Consider Paul's comments as he walked through the same process:

For I joyfully concur with the law of God in the inner man, but I see a different law in the members of my body, waging war against the law of my mind and making me a prisoner of the law of sin which is in my members. Wretched man that I am! Who will set me free from the body of this death? —Romans 7:22-24

Now that you have a backdrop of what God has accomplished through Christ, let's take a look at how you and I can begin to live out what He has already done within us. Paul expressed the frustrating clashes between the disparity of truth and our experience—but God also clearly presents us with the answer to the question, "Who will set me free from this roller coaster?"

Reclaiming Your Core Journal
Chapter 8 Thoughts, Questions & Insights

CHAPTER 9
Living the Impossible

L iving in and by the Spirit.

Before I started the process of getting back into shape, I was hovering around 205 pounds. Considering my height, I was well into the overweight category.

But after five months, I'd lost over 45 pounds—equating to losing about 50 pounds of fat and putting on around 10 pounds of muscle, per my estimations.

Do you know how much weight I tried to lose as a part of my fitness goals? None.

I had tried to lose weight in the past. For me, having a goal of losing weight was one of the most disappointing and discouraging experiences I've faced regarding my health. It'd seem like there was little reward for my effort. All of my gains were lost so easily by one week of falling off the wagon.

So I switched goals—which produced a completely different experience.

Losing weight wasn't my goal, nor was it my motivation. My goal was to increase my overall fitness. My motivation was being able to keep up with my grandkids for as long as I can. As I set my heart and effort on eating healthy and exercising, the weight loss became a byproduct—a highly welcomed byproduct, I might add.

When my attention turned to eating what was healthy, it kept me away from eating things that contained excessive amounts of calories and other ingredients that produced fat in my body. My focus on thorough, consistent exercise helped me utilize calories and build muscle.

Those dynamics are the same when it comes to living out the life of a believer.

Remember that biblical repentance is the process of coming into agreement with God's Word and combining it with faith. The fruit of repentance is a transformed life.

It isn't about calling attention to what you've done—but accepting what the Lord has done for you.

It's not about measuring how much sinful behavior you have in your life—it's about considering how much of what the Lord has provided you are currently living in and experiencing.

It's about shifting the focus of your heart—your thoughts and intents—from the things of this world to an alignment with the Holy Spirit. He takes things pertaining to Jesus Christ, revealing them to us. He teaches us to transition between the two.

This really needs to be said: In the natural, this is impossible. But thanks be to God, we don't live in the natural.

The book of Romans—chapter 8:1-15—is one of the clearest summaries of this process, revealing powerful keys to living a resurrected life.

Therefore there is now no condemnation for those who are in Christ Jesus. For the law of the Spirit of life in Christ Jesus has set you free from the law of sin and of death. For what the Law could not do, weak as it was through the flesh, God did: sending His Own Son in the likeness of sinful flesh and as an offering for sin, He condemned sin in the flesh, so that the requirement of the Law might be fulfilled in us, who do not walk according to the flesh but according to the Spirit. —Romans 8:1-4

I love how Paul leads with the fact that we who are in Christ are free from condemnation. This process that we're going through has nothing to do with sin or our fallen nature. Our exposure to the standard of righteousness in Christ isn't about making us feel bad for not measuring up.

In truth, if we're still struggling with feelings of guilt, shame, or condemnation—we haven't come to an understanding of what God has done in us.

In 1999, I was just entering into one of the most difficult times of my life. I had just stepped out of pastoral ministry and was trying to salvage my marriage of sixteen years that was collapsing. I felt like a complete failure because everything I'd worked so hard to build and preserve was falling apart.

One day, sitting at my desk, I pondered how worthless I was since I wasn't teaching, preaching, or pastoring. I wasn't counseling. I had no more disciples. I wasn't leading any Bible studies or group meetings. No outreach, no ministry. I considered myself a failure as a husband, father, pastor, and person. In my eyes, I really was worthless.

A few days later, the Lord asked me a question out of the blue.

"Son, where do you receive your value?"

Of course, I knew the right answer and quickly responded, "Lord, my value comes from your Son."

Then He asked me another question that broke through the haze of my destructive thought patterns.

"If your value comes from Me, then how could you be worthless because you're not doing anything for Me?"

My feelings of condemnation and worthlessness were a direct result of the lack of understanding regarding what He had done for me and who I already was in Him.

My value was determined by the price paid for me—not by the merit of my own efforts.

The first several verses of Romans 8 summarize what we've covered in the previous chapters, regarding our former identification with fallen humanity and, more importantly, our participation in the death and resurrection of Jesus Christ. We couldn't measure up to the Law, nor could we do anything to expunge the curse and penalty of our sin—so it was done for us.

In order to understand the process of growing in Christ, we must understand the triune nature of our lives. Paul talks about two paths that lay before us. One is the way of the flesh; the other is of the Spirit. The true essence of our being exists in our soul. It's that part of us that holds our mind, our will, and our emotions. Our thoughts, desires, and feelings are what make us who we are. It's the soul that holds the power to decide how we will live our life. The flesh is the physical container that holds and follows the instructions of our soul. The spirit is that part of us that is joined to and becomes one with God when we believe and receive Him.

But the one who joins himself to the Lord is one spirit with Him. —1 Corinthians 6:17

In Ephesians 2:5-6, we see that our spirit has already been perfected and is sitting with Christ at the right hand of the Father. The work of the cross and power of the resurrection are already complete in our spirit—there is nothing left to be done. Our soul, on the other hand, is in a process called sanctification.

God's Glossary
Sanctification (Strong's G0038): hagiasmós (hag-ee-as-mos). Gen. hagiasmoú. Masculine noun from hagiázō (hag-ee-ad-zo, Strong's G0037), meaning to sanctify. It's a sanctification, separation unto God. The resultant state of such a separation or the behavior befitting those so separated.

In simple terms, sanctification is the process of separating ourselves from the works of the flesh to a life of the Spirit. It's being set apart for God. As we live in and by the Spirit, we walk in what was accomplished for us "so that the requirement of the Law might be fulfilled in us, who do not walk according to the flesh but according to the Spirit."

There is a critical piece of information within that text that we must not miss. It's the fact that all efforts in the flesh—both good and bad—are the same.

I've spent decades in pursuit of the Lord. Much of that effort was directed toward becoming a good person. I worked hard to do the right things and avoid the wrong. That was both frustrating and exhausting. I had expended myself, trying to make my flesh conform to the standards of God's Word. But time and time again, I'd slip back into those old patterns and struggles.

Then the Lord opened my eyes to the reality that my flesh will never get on board with the Spirit. Any attempts to convince my flesh to be godly are completely futile. Notice how Paul clearly explains the dynamics of the flesh:

> **For those who are according to the flesh set their minds on the things of the flesh, but those who are according to the Spirit, the things of the Spirit. For the mind set on the flesh is death, but the mind set on the Spirit is life and peace, because the mind set on the flesh is hostile toward God; for it does not subject itself to the law of God, for it is not even able to do so, and those who are in the flesh cannot please God. —Romans 8:5-8**

When I realized there was nothing I could do to cause my flesh to conform to God's will, I felt a huge burden lift off my shoulders. I'm not called to try to be good—I'm called to die, that is, cease to exist to my fleshly nature.

Notice the key in this passage is about where you *set your mind*. Remember that the principle of repentance is to change your mind, which results in a change in your behavior.

> **By fixing our minds on the things of the Spirit, we direct the attention of our soul to the source of life and peace. In turn, that source begins to produce the life of the Spirit in our thoughts and actions.**

In 2000, within just several months' time, I'd gone through a divorce, the death of my dad following his prolonged battle with cancer, and the collapse of my company. Every area of my life that I'd spent years building lay around me in rubble. My marriage, ministry, business, and my network of relationships were in rubble. I was spiritually, mentally, and emotionally devastated.

Following that, I'd entered a time of deep brokenness and depression, regularly engaged in a struggle with thoughts of suicide. During that time, I found it increasingly difficult to maintain relationships and began to fear connection with anyone except my children.

Living in fear and pain with a fierce desire for self-preservation made having healthy relationships a virtual impossibility. As the relational wreckage began to pile up, I cried out to the Lord to do whatever He had to do in me to set me free from what was destroying my life.

The Lord heard me and began bringing me through an extended season of confronting those areas of my heart and mind that were holding on to a lie—then replacing that lie with the truth.

One of the first lies He exposed was the idea that I needed to be good in order to come to Him.

My heart was swirling with hate and anger, which I knew was wrong. I fought and struggled to forgive and get my anger under control, but it was like trying to hold a beach ball under water. You can hold it for a while, even until the surface of the water is calm, but there is always a pressure. It continues to build until you slip—and it gushes out all over the place, over anyone that's close to you.

I tried and tried to overcome the rage until one day the Lord encouraged me to invite the Holy Spirit into my hate and unforgiveness. What? Invite Him into that disgusting place? That made no sense to my self-righteous mind at all.

Up to that point, I had believed the lie that my failure made me unworthy of God's love and deserving of His punishment. I had believed that God only accepted those who were behaving in a manner consistent with His will.

At that moment, I was confronted with the truth that my right standing with Him—accomplished by the death of His Son—had nothing to do with what I deserved. It was His blood that removed my sin and made me righteous.

Of course, all believers know that to be true. So this truth wasn't new to me— I had readily accepted it as truth many years earlier. The difference was that now I saw the conflict. I was made aware that even though I had acknowledged God's payment for my sin, there was an area in my heart that was holding on to something that was incongruent with that truth.

That is where I had to make a choice. Who would I believe? Would I continue holding to the lie that I had to be clean before the Lord would inhabit an area of my life? Or would I believe His Word and invite Him into the dark, twisted mess of my heart?

Think of it this way. Your soul stands as the authority between your flesh and your spirit. When you're born again, your spirit is already one with the Lord and abides in the fullness of Christ. Your spirit always lives in complete agreement with the Law and desires of the Father. Your flesh loves the world and the things of the world. It finds comfort in sin and having its own way. It doesn't want the things of God—it only wants whatever will gratify the desire of the moment. Your soul gets to decide where you will put your attention and with whom you will agree.

If you choose to agree with your spirit, you will allow that life to be expressed through your soul. If you choose to agree with the flesh, then that's what will be expressed.

> **However, you are not in the flesh but in the Spirit, if indeed the Spirit of God dwells in you. But if anyone does not have the Spirit of Christ, he does not belong to Him. If Christ is in you, though the body is dead because of sin, yet the spirit is alive because of righteousness. But if the Spirit of Him who raised Jesus from the dead dwells in you, He who raised Christ Jesus from the dead will also give life to your mortal bodies through His Spirit who dwells in you. —Romans 8:9-11**

—〰—

Spirit-led vs. religion

In my experience, I would have to say that one of the greatest stumbling blocks to living a spirit-led life is religion.

Religion, at its core, is our attempt to be good and earn God's favor and acceptance. It's basically a list of dos and don'ts that function as a standard for measuring our lives.

Anything I feel I must do to be acceptable to the Lord is rooted in the flesh and religion. The flip side of the same coin is when I feel that my behavior can diminish my standing before the Lord. This is *self*-righteousness. Anything I do or don't do that I attempt to use as a measurement of my righteousness is a work of the flesh—including reading the Bible, praying, going to church, sharing my faith, etc.

Let me be careful here to explain that *what* I do, in and of itself, is not the issue. To be sure, there is nothing wrong with reading, praying, etc.

The problem comes when I believe that I need to do those things in order to be okay with the Lord.

To state it as directly to you as I can, your righteousness was given to you apart from your effort. You can't add to it, neither can you take away from it.

Your righteousness is a settled issue in heaven and in your spirit. To place merit on your own efforts is a work of the flesh, which isn't pleasing to the Lord. In fact, I believe to do so is an insult to the cross and the height of arrogance. It's declaring to the Father that His provision for your sin was insufficient and needs your fleshly efforts to be completed. To hold on to an argument that your sin can diminish your righteousness is to say your ability to sin outweighs His ability to atone and that He needs your assistance.

The truth is that "He made Him who knew no sin to be sin on our behalf, so that we might become the righteousness of God in Him," per 1 Corinthians 5:21.

You *are* the righteousness of God in Christ Jesus.

So then, brethren, we are under obligation, not to the flesh, to live according to the flesh—for if you are living according to the flesh, you must die; but if by the Spirit you are putting to death the deeds of the body, you will live. For all who are being led by the Spirit of God, these are sons of God. For you have not received a spirit of slavery leading to fear again, but you have received a spirit of adoption as sons by which we cry out, Abba! Father! —Romans 8:12-15

Think of yourself—that is, your soul—as a garden hose. What flows in you and through you depends on which faucet you're connected to. If you're connected to a water faucet, you'll be filled with water and it will flow through you. If you're connected to a toxic waste faucet, that is what will flow in and through you.

Anything you believe you must do to attain or achieve the Christian life originates from the flesh and has no ability to accomplish anything of value. Instead, you're called to fix your mind and align your thoughts and agreement with the truth that the work has already been done, and you're complete in Christ. When you do that, you allow the life that is already in you to express itself through your soul—thoughts, desires, and emotions.

The flesh is compelled to strive toward righteousness. The spirit lives in righteousness and expresses what has already been done.

Herein lies the beauty and power of your life in the Lord. No longer do you live a life based on an unattainable standard of dos and don'ts. You live in a moment-by-moment relationship with the One who lives in you.

Throughout each day, I encounter dozens of opportunities to lean into the completed work inside me or to partner with my flesh. Each time I choose to stand with my spirit, I deny my flesh, putting it to death and releasing the fragrance of Christ into the world around me.

That may sound like an oversimplification of our walk with the Lord, but I assure you it's that simple. Not always easy, but simple. Our one task is simply to listen to the Spirit and follow Him, allowing His abundant life to flow in and through us. He will never lead us into sin, but will always lead us into the fullness of our destiny in Him. The supernatural byproduct of focusing on cultivating our relationship with the Lord will be life, peace, and joy. You won't have to try to produce this fruit. It'll grow on its own because by fixing your eyes on Him you are being transformed into all that you were created to be.

This is the step-by-step process of bringing every area of your life into agreement with the truth of who you are in Him. When you encounter an area of your thoughts or belief systems that are in opposition to who He says you are, reject the lie and choose the truth. You're not living your life in front of a judge who is weighing the good and bad of your efforts—but walking from childhood to adulthood, hand-in-hand with a loving Father.

A Father who teaches and trains you, corrects and disciplines, and prepares you for your purpose in His family.

Reclaiming your core comes as a byproduct of having a transformed mind. Understanding the anatomy of a renewed mind will help you engage more effectively in this process. Let's take a leap into the dynamics of a mind that's being renewed.

Reclaiming Your Core Journal
Chapter 9 Thoughts, Questions & Insights

CHAPTER 10

Anatomy of a Renewed Mind

U nderstanding the physical dynamics of your human anatomy is an important aspect of getting into shape. Some things work and some don't.

You can exert a lot of effort with very little result if you're unaware of either the potential or the limitations of your body. You need to know how your body responds to food and exercise to minimize wasted effort and function at your peak.

For the past several years, I've been working as a project management consultant in the healthcare industry at multiple hospital systems across the US. I'm an application analyst with a certification in Advanced Project Management. My job entails going into an organization, analyzing the current state of processes and procedures, and with that information, constructing a potential future state design. Upon approval, I work to build, test, and implement solutions that streamline, improve, or optimize those workflows.

Every organization I've worked with has been different. The people, the problems, and the places have been unique. Even though I've no idea what I will encounter when I show up on a new project, I'm able to enter that unknown environment and provide actionable solutions.

The key to success in situations like this is to realize that I don't need to know how or why things are the way they are. I just need to know what is possible. Because I know what is possible, I view everything through that paradigm.

I see each workflow through the eyes of what it can be—not what it is.

Reclaiming the core of our identity is similar in many ways. So many fundamental truths in the foundations of our faith are systematic and predictable. That's why the Lord was able to teach in parables. Parables illustrate patterns and processes that help us to understand the dynamics of our relationship with Him and how His kingdom functions.

Let's take a few moments here to consider the patterns and processes regarding the renewal of the mind. Even though we'll be reviewing some of the foundational information discussed previously, my goal is to illustrate the process that can be applied to any truth as it pertains to our life in the kingdom of God.

Each of us is different, and there are many unknowns in the journey before us. The key is in knowing what is possible. With every unknown area of our heart the Lord leads us into, we can apply the same principles and processes illustrated in the first steps we took in our relationship with the Lord.

Consider your first steps as a new believer. You were living a life of sin, darkness, and self-centeredness, then someone spoke the truth to you about Jesus Christ and what He did for you on the cross. You had a choice at that moment to agree with and accept this new thought and combine it with faith—or to dismiss it and continue in agreement with what you believed about life up to that point. When you agreed with the truth and combined it with faith, it produced a change in you. Your outlook shifted, and your eyes were opened to see a whole world you previously had been blinded from seeing.

Let's take a look at a passage from Romans that speaks specifically of the promise and process of salvation, where each of us began our walk with the Lord:

But what does it say? "The word is near you, in your mouth and in your heart"—that is, the word of faith which we are

preaching, that if you confess with your mouth Jesus as Lord, and believe in your heart that God raised Him from the dead, you will be saved; for with the heart a person believes, resulting in righteousness, and with the mouth he confesses, resulting in salvation. —Romans 10:8-10

Breaking this passage down, we see several things. The first is to *confess* Jesus as Lord.

To confess speaks of coming into agreement and consenting—in this case, consenting to the lordship of Jesus Christ in your life. This isn't simply the mental assent of acknowledging a title to the Messiah. (If that was the case, then even demons and satan could be saved since "every knee will bow and tongue confess that Jesus Christ is Lord.") This confession refers to the positional agreement regarding your relationship to the Lord. Within that statement, you can see the process of transformation at work.

The truth that Jesus Christ is Lord is now combined with your agreement, which causes a change in your belief from Jesus Christ being a Lord to being *your* Lord.

If, in fact, you acknowledge and consent to Jesus Christ as your master, ruler, Lord, and God, then you're aligning yourself with the implications of that revelation. Let me put it another way. If I'm agreeing that someone is my boss, then I'm acknowledging that when s/he says I should do something, I do it. When the person communicates an expectation that I don't do something, I don't do it. From that point on, I am no longer my own.

Next, there is a belief—which is the combining of truth with faith—that God raised Him from the dead. Before we look at the anatomy of this part of the process, let's pause for a moment and look at some specifics regarding the significance of Jesus Christ being raised from the dead and why it's an absolute component of salvation.

Firstly, we must acknowledge that in order for there to be a resurrection, there needs to be a death. In the case of our Savior, it was the death of the perfect sacrifice, a shedding of His sinless blood, without which there can be no forgiveness. In order for us to be free from the penalty of sin, someone had to pay the price of it. The penalty for sin is death—and by shedding His blood, Jesus Christ satisfied the debt with the Father.

Now that the price for sin has been paid, only the one who paid that price has the right to take issue with it. To further clarify, no one—including you—has a right to be your judge. Only Jesus can do that and He is actually interceding on our behalf. Having already paid the price for sin, He has no interest in revisiting it with you who belong to and believe in Him.

Secondly, as it relates to the resurrection—without it we have no power or ability to live the life that was purchased for us. Jesus' death covers our past, but the resurrection opens the door for our future fellowship with the Father.

Even though our sins were forgiven, there is still an absolute standard of holiness with the Father. Jesus' death paid for our sinful behavior, but the expectation of righteousness was not lowered—it's still far beyond our reach.

Per Romans, chapters 6 through 8, if we've been identified with Christ in His death—which acknowledges the provision of His sacrifice for our sin and our agreement to leave the kingdom of darkness and enter into alignment with and submission to His lordship in the *Kingdom of Light*—then we'll also be raised up with Him in newness of life to live according to that life that now dwells in us.

Therefore there is now no condemnation for those who are in Christ Jesus. For the law of the Spirit of life in Christ Jesus has set you free from the law of sin and of death. For what the Law could not do, weak as it was through the flesh, God did: sending His Own Son in the likeness of sinful flesh and as an offering for sin, He condemned sin in the flesh, so that the requirement of the Law might be fulfilled in us, who do not walk according to the flesh but according to the Spirit. —Romans 8:1-4

The resurrection of Jesus Christ forever satisfies the Father's standard of righteousness. As you and I walk in Him—by the same Spirit that raised Him—we live, move, and have our being in Him. Now joined with Him, we have been given His righteousness. We can never add to or take away from what has been given.

Now let's get back to Romans 10. Notice the clear expression of repentance at work in verse 10—"for with the heart a person believes, resulting in righteousness and with the mouth confesses, resulting in salvation." We can see that when we agree, consent, and align our beliefs with faith, there is a corresponding effect.

Think of it this way: God's Word is the seed, and your believing heart is the fertile soil. When those two things are combined, the corresponding result will be the development and fruitfulness of the seed's potential. There is nothing the soil could do to create or fabricate the plant, much less any fruit. It's simply the recipient and container of a life that draws on the available nutrients. The nutrient you provide is your faith.

Notice the core elements of this process. Your heart is positioned to receive the truth. When you hear the truth, you decide if you'll reject it or receive it by faith. The truth will always expose the lie, just as light reveals what's in darkness. In each case, you'll choose to reject the lie you held on to prior to being presented with the truth. From that point forward, you'll hold on to and nurture the truth in the soil of your heart, which absolutely will bear fruit and increase. This is the anatomy of the renewing-of-the-mind process.

Now if you take this same principle and apply it to the truths and commandments of Jesus Christ, you'll find He will transform every area of your life. Here's one of the clearest passages speaking about that.

Therefore I urge you, brethren, by the mercies of God, to present your bodies a living and holy sacrifice, acceptable to God, which is your spiritual service of worship. And do not be conformed to this world, but be transformed by the *renewing of your mind*, so that you may prove what the will of God is, that which is good and acceptable and perfect. —Romans 12:1-2

When you renew your mind, you'll be transformed. Conversely, changing your behavior will do nothing to bring about true transformation. You may learn to play the parts, but you'll not become the person you were created to be any more than actors become the characters they portray.

—⋙—

Repeating the process

To illustrate the ongoing process of transforming our minds, let's carry the analogy of the soil a little farther: Your soul, that is your heart and mind, is a field. This field is full of rocks, weeds, and debris. Someone bought the field and gave you a bag of seed, a helper, and the responsibility to tend and care for the field.

In caring for the field, you would begin by removing the debris, rocks, and weeds. Then you'd prepare the soil by fertilizing and tilling it, and go on to plant the seeds. The field would need to be protected, watered, and monitored for any weeds trying to return and encroach on your crops. All the while you're taking care of the field, you're aware that one day the owner will come and expect to receive the harvest.

The same process you would go through as a good steward of this field is the same process you are called to follow regarding your life. You were purchased by the precious blood of Jesus Christ and given the compassionate Holy Spirit to come alongside you to help in this process of preparation, planting, and tending the garden of your heart. You've been given His Word and His promise that there will come a time when He will return to receive back what He has purchased.

Each thought process or belief contrary to God's Word is a weed that can never produce anything but seeds that will multiply negative influence in your life. The only way to stop the multiplication of weeds in your life is to remove them, replacing them with the seed of God's Word, the truth.

Trying to change yourself is like trying to get weeds to produce wheat.

Regardless of the nobility of your intentions, it just won't work. Consider the instruction of the Lord through the prophet Isaiah:

Seek the Lord while He may be found; Call upon Him while He is near. Let the wicked forsake his way and the unrighteous man his thoughts; and let him return to the Lord, and He will have compassion on him, and to our God, for He will abundantly pardon. "For My thoughts are not your thoughts, nor

are your ways My ways," declares the Lord. "For as the heavens are higher than the earth, so are My ways higher than your ways and My thoughts than your thoughts." —Isaiah 55:6-9

Renewal of the mind is not the process of dealing with sin—it's the process of applying the promises and provisions of the Lord Jesus Christ into your daily life.

It's the process of finding freedom from the entanglements and encumbrances of this world.
It's the healing of past and present emotional wounds.
It's the path to growing up into the fullness of what was purchased for you on the cross.
In essence, it's simply discovering the truth, agreeing with it, and consenting to and aligning with that truth.

The freedom that comes from a renewed mind will position you, me, and every believer to be victorious in the battles we'll face in this world. Yes, the life of the Spirit is a battle. It's a battle where we're engaging internal and external forces that are at odds with the fullness that has been made available in Christ. It's a battle for the truth.

We will need weapons to identify and demolish enemy strongholds and reclaim what rightfully belongs to us.

—⚕—

Reclaiming Your Core Journal
Chapter 10 Thoughts, Questions & Insights

CHAPTER 11
Engaged in Battle

The number one lesson in the pursuit of health and fitness: Don't quit. You will face challenges—and there will be times that your body will dig the heels in and push back. It's in these moments that you'll need to pull on the strength you have inside.

There also will be difficult times as you reclaim your spiritual core. One dark night in the midst of a season of brokenness, I was pounded by a crisis in my soul. I was hurting. I was alone. I wanted the pain to stop and sleep to come. Neither did.

What did come was the overwhelming thought that I didn't want to live like this anymore. I was repeatedly assaulted with the compulsion to go and retrieve my handgun. Over and over again, the thought came. "Just go get it. You know you're not going to do anything with it. Just go get it to prove to yourself that you can do it." I found no sleep that night as the voice relentlessly pounded my thoughts with the same plea.

Even though I was at a crisis point in my life—which was in many ways, a new beginning—I knew enough to realize that if I gave in to the first request, it would be followed by another and another. Each would lead me closer to one inevitable end. My enemy was out to kill me.

It was a battle. And in no uncertain terms, life and death hung in the balance. The battleground was my mind, and the weapons of the enemy were empowered by my thoughts and beliefs. My only defense at that time was that I had begun to learn the truth—which was enough to keep me from playing into the ignorance I was under at the time.

To become a skilled warrior in this battle, I had a lot to learn.

As a new creation, we're called to learn everything anew. The problem is that our natural man doesn't like it and constantly tries to apply the same thought processes and principles of the old life to the new. The old ways—the ways of the flesh and the world—have no relevance in the life of the Spirit. Not only do they have no relevance, they are literally and diametrically opposed to the ways of the Spirit. The ways of the flesh and the world intentionally, often in cooperation with the enemy, do violence to our precious new life. The only hope we truly have to walk in this new life is to change our thought processes by the acceptance of God's work and His Word.

In Romans 8, we see the backdrop of the battle between the flesh and the spirit. In this world, our flesh finds allies in the realms of darkness and in the spirit of this world. Since our flesh is never in agreement with the Holy Spirit, it will readily agree with those forces that will help it get its own way. The good news is the battle has already been won—our surpassing victory declared. The battle we wage is to lay claim to what is already ours.

For though we walk in the flesh, we do not war according to the flesh, for the weapons of our warfare are not of the flesh, but divinely powerful for the destruction of fortresses. We are destroying speculations and every lofty thing raised up against the knowledge of God, and we are taking every thought captive to the obedience of Christ. —2 Corinthians 10:3-5

In this passage we also see that there is a clear delineation between the efforts of the flesh and weapons that are divinely powerful. It can't be overstated that trying to overcome the flesh and the enemy in our own strength is a massive waste of time.

This battle is taking place in our thoughts, knowledge and beliefs. It's here that our fleshly nature works in conjunction with the world and with the enemy of our soul to build strongholds and fortresses that confront the truth of who God says He is and who we are in Him. The tactics of the flesh and the enemy are to get us to speculate on the whys and what-ifs. The goal is to forge walls of excuses built on human wisdom as to why we should not hold to the truth. The end result is that we'll elevate our perceived knowledge above God's Word.

The simplest terms to clarify this conflict? Understand we're confronting a lie with the truth. Any area of our life where we're experiencing less than the fullness of life, love, joy, and peace of the kingdom of God is the result of believing a lie. To engage and tear down these strongholds of deception in our soul, we must know the truth and realign our agreement to be consistent with Him.

The Lord used my battle with suicidal thoughts to illustrate the foundational skills I needed to confront this stronghold in my life.

At the source of the enemy's power was the fact that I was entertaining the idea that things would not get better. That no one loved me. That my life had no value. Even though I didn't believe these things to be true, I allowed those thoughts to become familiar. I found a false comfort in feeling sorry for myself and used them to justify looking to sources other than the Lord for security or validation.

Giving free reign to thoughts that conflict with God's truth empowers the enemy to leverage the carnal desires of our flesh and lead us into behaviors and decisions that will bring destruction in our lives. When left unchecked, these thoughts and ideas create strongholds, fortresses of thoughts that rob us of the fullness of life that is ours in Christ.

To destroy these fortresses, we must take our thoughts captive. We must restrict their ability to freely roam in our minds. Once we identify those thoughts and beliefs that try to exalt themselves above the knowledge of the Lord, we are to call a meeting between the Truth—who is Jesus Christ—and these thoughts. As the truth of God's Word confronts these thoughts and ideas, you and I have authority to force them to submit and to obey the Truth.

As the Spirit helped me to see the strongholds of thought I had developed, I was able to stop them from running rampant in my mind. I then took each thought process and replaced it with God's truth. The strongholds of defeat and self-pity were replaced by the strong tower of the truth that my Father loves me, and my future is filled with hope and the expectation of good things.

—〰—

Identifying strongholds

The process of finding these strongholds is straightforward. It's a natural byproduct of getting to know the Lord. The Lord Jesus gave this instruction to His disciples before He ascended to the Father:

> **All authority has been given to Me in heaven and on earth. Go therefore and make disciples of all the nations, baptizing them in the name of the Father and the Son and the Holy Spirit, teaching them to observe all that I commanded you; and lo, I am with you always, even to the end of the age. —Matthew 28:18-20**

The mandate to those who laid the foundation of the Church was to establish the things spoken by Jesus Christ. Therefore, anything built thereafter must be within the structural confines of that foundation. I'm stating the obvious for one reason—to clarify our focus as it pertains to the standard in which we're called to live.

As you and I surrender our lives to the Spirit and grow in our knowledge and understanding of Jesus Christ, we will be regularly confronted with the opportunity to compare what we believe against what God's Word states. Structures in our thoughts that are in conflict with the truth are the strongholds we must address. Within the process of demolishing these strongholds lays the opportunity to be transformed, as we bring our beliefs into agreement and alignment with the truth. Let's look at those Romans 12 verses again.

> **Therefore I urge you, brethren, by the mercies of God, to present your bodies a living and holy sacrifice, acceptable to God, which is your spiritual service of worship. And do not be conformed to this world but be transformed by the renewing of your mind, that you may prove what the will of God is, that which is good and acceptable and perfect. —Romans 12:1-2**

Do not be conformed to this world. The word for *conformed* in the Greek means to be fashioned according to a pattern. We're not called to pattern our lives according to the world or its ways. Instead of allowing ourselves to be pressed into the mold that the culture of the world and our flesh want us to be, we are to be transformed.

In this passage the Greek word for transformed is *metamorphoses* and speaks of being changed from one thing into something else. This transformational process takes place by confronting the lies and renewing our mind with the truth. This transformation takes place through our agreement with the truth.

Just like the journey to reclaim my physical core, the choice to agree with God's Word was much more difficult at the beginning of the process. Now that I have accumulated years of testimony experiencing the abundant life in Christ that comes from aligning with God's truth, it's much easier. I've come to fully expect that any idea, thought, or belief that stands in opposition to the Word is preventing me from experiencing something beautiful.

One of the most prevalent tactics I see the enemy effectively using is to get people to agree with the lie that their problems and challenges are the fault of someone or something else. That's the equivalent of blaming McDonald's for being overweight.

When we take ownership of what we allow into our lives and what we do with it, we'll come to understand that we have much more influence on the condition of our lives than we might suspect.

Since we've been given a free will, neither the lie nor the truth has any inherent power to force us to agree. The choice—as well as the consequence of the choice—is ours alone. This truth rips away every excuse for the condition of our circumstances while simultaneously empowering us to change our lives.

Remember, you release power and authority to what you agree with in your life—whether good or bad, truth or lie.

The focus of the battle

There is another important insight regarding the battle we're engaged in as we walk with the Lord. Notice the focus of this battle isn't the enemy—it's the truth.

In my battle for fitness, I focus on eating healthy and pursuing a balanced approach to cardiovascular and muscular training. Focusing on unhealthy things won't help. My goal is to remove anything that doesn't help me to advance my health and fitness goals. That pertains to everything, good or bad.

In my pursuit of a healthy walk with the Lord, I focus on God's truth and a balanced approach of applying what the Lord reveals to me. In some cases, my thoughts, beliefs, and subsequently, my actions need to be changed. My desire is to be transformed by the truth. To that end, I'm ready to bring my thoughts and beliefs into agreement with the truth. I strive to bring into balance—or if need be, completely cut away—anything good or bad that stands outside of, or in opposition to, the truth.

Therefore if you have been raised up with Christ, keep seeking the things above, where Christ is, seated at the right hand of God. Set your mind on the things above, not on the things that are on earth. For you have died and your life is hidden with Christ in God. When Christ, who is our life, is revealed, then you also will be revealed with Him in glory.

Therefore consider the members of your earthly body as dead to immorality, impurity, passion, evil desire, and greed, which amounts to idolatry. —Colossians 3:1-5

Regular, knowledge-based exercise is crucial for fitness, but without a healthy diet you will diminish, if not completely eliminate, the benefits of your investment. Two key ingredients for a healthy lifestyle are diet and exercise. Simple healthy choices regarding what you allow into your body—as well as what you keep out—will have huge benefits.

For me, I avoid extreme *diets* and focus on a balanced, well-portioned variety of natural, unprocessed foods combined with some baseline supplements to make sure the basics are covered. Not only have I lost weight, but I've gained energy and endurance to push my body to a greater level of fitness than ever before.

Do you know that it's possible to get overweight by eating healthy food? There needs to be a balance of intake—physically, as well as spiritually. Some spiritual food may taste great, but unless it's combined with faith and agreement, which produce action, it just turns into fat.

As we consider our spiritual fitness, we can apply the same principle—eating a balanced diet (agreeing with the truth) and exercise (applying the truth) will produce the greatest return on our efforts.

When we lay the foundation for our belief system—or, in many of our cases, when we re-clarify our foundation—we must rely on a core diet of natural, organic, unprocessed food for our soul. What I mean by processed is anything that's been filtered through another human being. Teaching, preaching, books (including this one), tapes, sermons, articles, etc. must all be secondary to the core focus of our own experience with the Word of God, by the revelation of the Holy Spirit. The Spirit is more than able to give you understanding and revelation regarding the truth.

We might use some *supplements* to help us at various times, but the ingredient list needs to be verified. Sometimes we find—in the natural and the spiritual—there are many processed ingredients that aren't healthy, but have been added to food that's supposed to be good for us. The solution is to learn to read the labels.

Spiritually speaking, we need to know the Word of God for ourselves. The Holy Spirit will teach us what we need to know. As we supplement our diet with what the Lord shares through other believers, we will become increasingly aware of what's not based on the truth and what comes as a result of an organic relationship with the Lord.

Now that we have reviewed the overall process of engaging the lies in contrast to the truth, let's look at some practical steps to applying these core truths in our lives. It's time to go on the offensive.

Reclaiming Your Core Journal
Chapter 11 Thoughts, Questions & Insights

CHAPTER 12
Counter-Offensive

Becoming physically fit isn't the end game—it's the starting point of a lifestyle. Once you become fit, the goal is to keep what you have and add to it. To maintain a healthy lifestyle, you'll need to apply what you've learned and build on the basics as you develop and mature.

For your spiritual man, the foundation has been set and the offer has been made. The Spirit is tugging on your heart to embrace this life that has been purchased for you. Your first step is to accept the invitation and to accept the exchange:

Your life for His.

Your sin and selfishness for a life of obedience to His voice, His purpose, and His plan for your life.

This is no simple prayer, nor is it a one-time event. It's surrendering your life, not living for yourself. It's the acknowledgment that you're not the lord of your life—He is.

Committing your life to Jesus Christ is not meant to be an easy decision that passes by with heads bowed and an arm slipped up in silence. It's meant to be a reckoning—as a king preparing for war with life and death hanging in the balance.

It's like a builder considering the cost of time and materials before beginning the construction of his home. This step, if done correctly, will be an unshakable foundation for building a structure that will take the rest of your life to complete.

If that isn't the process you went through at the beginning of your walk, then now is the time to revisit that decision. Anything less is a cheap imitation of what was offered to you by the Lord. His offer hasn't changed. If you want to be His disciple, you must deny yourself, take up your cross every day—the cross is the place where you die daily—and follow Him in the example He gave.

I made that decision over 37 years ago. I've faced trials, tragedies, and more correction than I could even begin to remember. And I've faced many opportunities to abandon the life of denying my fleshly and carnal impulses, and partake of all that this world and the god of this world have to offer. I can tell you without equivocation—I wouldn't trade one moment of the worst that I've faced for the Lord for a lifetime of the best that this world and all the powers of hell have to offer. I serve a God who loves me and has only my good in mind. I'll give up anything and everything that He asks of me because my life doesn't belong to me, it belongs to Him.

This invitation isn't a sales pitch. It's not a promise of an easier life. It's an invitation to die to what you thought you would or could be and to embrace the design of the One who created you.

To be sure, there is an eternal reward for those who accept—and the assurance of the direst of consequence for those who don't. But we'll discuss that shortly.

This is the promise: Jesus Christ has paid the price so you could be restored into fellowship with the Father in the fullness of all that was available to humanity before the fall. You'll be given grace, forgiveness, and power through the Holy Spirit to walk through this process—no matter how long it might take. The Lord won't give up on you or hold any of your failures against you.

—⟶⟶⟶—

Hide God's Word in your heart

The Word of God is truly seed. You can be sure that if you regularly take time to get His Word in your heart and mind, it will bear fruit. Over the years, I've employed many different methods to get to know the Lord through the Bible.

Here are some of the things I've done that might give you some ideas:

- Read through the Bible in a year, following reading programs.
- Slowly work through books of the Bible, reading only a few verses at a time and then spend all day thinking about them.
- Listen to the Bible in audio format.
- Watch videos that read the Bible verbatim.
- Take turns reading books of the Bible with your spouse, friend, or with a group.
- Read Proverbs in a month, one chapter at a time, corresponding to the day's date—e.g. on the fifth of the month read Proverbs 5, etc.
- Read Psalms in a month by reading every 30th Psalm based on the day's date—on the fifth of the month read Psalms 5, 35, 65, 95, and 125.
- Read through a book of the Bible in multiple translations. Some of my favorites are New American Standard Bible, New Living Translation, and The Amplified Bible. My wife and I've been reading The Tree of Life Version and passages from The Message and The Passion Translation.

All Scripture is inspired by God and profitable for teaching, for reproof, for correction, for training in righteousness; so that the man of God may be adequate, equipped for every good work. —2 Timothy 3:16-17

As you read and ponder God's Word, invite the Holy Spirit to speak to you. He will show you the truth and expose any lies you believe. Just like in any relationship, it's a good idea to spend regular time in fellowship with the Holy Spirit through the Word.

Learn to recognize the works of the flesh

It is helpful to have an awareness of how your flesh operates when it is having its own way. The book of Galatians contains a good example of what it looks like when we're not being led by the Spirit.

But I say, walk by the Spirit, and you will not carry out the desire of the flesh. For the flesh sets its desire against the Spirit, and the Spirit against the flesh; for these are in opposition to one another, so that you may not do the things that you please. But if you are led by the Spirit, you are not under the Law. Now the deeds of the flesh are evident, which are: immorality, impurity, sensuality, idolatry, sorcery, enmities, strife, jealousy, outbursts of anger, disputes, dissensions, factions, envying, drunkenness, carousing, and things like these, of which I forewarn you, just as I have forewarned you, that those who practice such things will not inherit the kingdom of God. —Galatians 5:16-21

As shared previously, when I was consistently struggling with anger, I knew something was out of agreement with the Spirit. I clearly could see that anger was identified as a deed of the flesh—and that was the beginning of a process where the Lord delivered me from that stronghold. That's one example of why it is important to be able to recognize the works of the flesh. When you see deeds of the flesh manifesting in your life, it's an invitation to start a conversation with the Lord to find out why they are there.

It's important to realize that this passage in Galatians 5 isn't a list of don'ts. It's a deeds-of-the-flesh list. These deeds are like lights on the dashboard of your car. When that red light that looks like an oil can shows up, it isn't a rebuke. It's a notification that something needs attention. So it is with the items on this list. Think of them as your *flesh-lights*.

If you're regularly experiencing immorality, impurity, and sensuality in your life, then you can be sure there is an area of your soul cooperating with the flesh and the enemy. These behaviors are an indicator that there is a stronghold the Lord wants to help you destroy so you can live in the fullness of joy He purchased for you.

Likewise, strife, jealousy, anger, division, or any of the other deeds of the flesh are an invitation to work through the process of repentance with the Spirit and the Word. It's the work of transforming your mind that will lead to freedom.

—\\\—

Learn to recognize the fruit of the spirit

On the flip side of the spectrum is the process of growing familiar with what it looks and feels like when we're walking in agreement with the Holy Spirit and our true nature in Christ.

> **But the fruit of the Spirit is love, joy, peace, patience, kindness, goodness, faithfulness, gentleness, self-control; against such things there is no law. Now those who belong to Christ Jesus have crucified the flesh with its passions and desires. If we live by the Spirit, let us also walk by the Spirit. Let us not become boastful, challenging one another, envying one another. —Galatians 5:22-26**

When you're walking in the atmosphere of heaven, you will experience various aspects of the fruit of the Spirit as listed in Galatians 5. Once again, this isn't a list of dos that you try to perform—that would be works. Instead, these attributes are evidence of the Holy Spirit's presence in your life. It's the fruit that reveals that you're walking in agreement with the Holy Spirit. It is the result of the process of receiving the Word by faith, allowing it to transform you. A life transformed by the Spirit produces results in your soul.

Recognizing the fruit of the Spirit in your life can also help you identify areas that aren't in agreement with the truth. For example, if there's an area of your life where you're not experiencing self-control, you can be sure there is something out of agreement with the kingdom of God. Every area of our life that is in agreement with the truth of God's Word and in alignment with the Holy Spirit will exhibit the fruit of the Spirit.

Personally, I found it very helpful to memorize Galatians 5:22-26. I often use this passage to consider . . .

Do I see clear evidence of God's love in my life?
Am I experiencing joy?
Is my heart at rest in His peace?
Am I exhibiting a long-suffering patience with others and in my circumstances?
Is there evidence of kindness, goodness, and gentleness?
Am I bearing the fruit of faithfulness?
Is my behavior in line with a lifestyle of self-control—or am I easily pulled off course into destructive behavior?

In instances where I may be lacking, I don't attempt to do better. For example, if I am lacking peace in my circumstances, I make no attempt to make myself peaceful. Instead I ask the Holy Spirit, "What lie am I holding on to that is preventing your fruit from being expressed in this area of my life?"

What is the difference between works and fruit? Works are the results of your efforts. Fruit is a by-product of the right combination of elements.

My wife and I were having lunch at some friends'. In the center of the table was a large wooden bowl filled with beautiful fruit. I reached to grab a peach and realized it was fake. The craftsmanship of that fruit was amazing—I literally thought it was a peach. It even had realistic blemishes and discoloration. As I looked at the fruit, I heard the Lord speak to my heart: "This is what religion produces."

Religion—or in other words, our own efforts—can do nothing more than make things that look like fruit. The fruit of our relationship with the Lord isn't something we have to work for any more than a peach has to work at becoming a peach. If we're properly connected to the Lord, bringing our thoughts and beliefs into agreement with His Word, we will produce the fruit of the Spirit.

Agree quickly with God's Word
Confess your sin to God and your peers in the Lord

When God's Word confronts your thoughts and behaviors, make a conscious decision that His Word will take precedence over your own thoughts, actions, and/or beliefs. If God calls a certain behavior/attitude sin—then call it sin.

John's letter as recorded in 1 John is a powerful resource filled with helpful insights for your walk. I would recommend spending some time with the Spirit reviewing this passage. In chapter one, there is a key verse the Lord has used to unlock the power of His blood in my life:

If we confess our sins, He is faithful and righteous to forgive us our sins and to cleanse us from all unrighteousness. —1 John 1:9

Remember that to confess is to acknowledge and agree with what we're confessing. In this passage, we see our part and God's part in the process of dealing with the sinful behavior in our life. Our part: We agree with God. What He calls sin, we call sin. Now look at His part: He is faithful and righteous to forgive and cleanse us of all unrighteousness.

As you allow the Spirit and the Word to convict you of sin, your part is to say, "Yes, Lord. I agree this isn't Your best for me, and it misses the mark for all You've intended for my life. This isn't part of who You've called and created me to be, and I don't want any part of it."

When you do that, He forgives you and takes responsibility to cleanse that out of your life. Remember that through your agreement with His Word, you're breaking your agreement and alignment with the thoughts and beliefs that produced that behavior in your life. Instead, you're agreeing and aligning yourself with the truth of what He has declared. This, in turn, produces fruit in your life.

Through your confession, the power of sin is destroyed in your life. However, there are times when destructive behavior will continue to manifest. In those cases, you must continue to seek the Lord regarding your belief systems surrounding that behavior.

There are often areas of our lives that are built on strongholds, which are connected with multiple lies or misconceptions. These are dismantled over time and by process.

—⟋⟍—

Don't get discouraged in the journey

I can assure you, there are many areas of your heart that are dark and sinful when exposed to the light of Jesus Christ. This is a natural part of the process of being conformed to His image. Stand fast on the truth that you're already righteous in Him, and He is prepared to walk with you through the process of sanctifying your soul.

—⟋⟍—

Continue to train your brain

It takes repetition over time to learn anything new. Retraining your brain to agree with God's Word is no different. Don't give up. Don't allow discouragement to keep you from all that has been prepared for you. Once again, those Romans 12 verses lead the way.

> **Therefore I urge you, brethren, by the mercies of God, to present your bodies a living and holy sacrifice, acceptable to God, which is your spiritual service of worship. And do not be conformed to this world but be transformed by the renewing of your mind, that you may prove what the will of God is, that which is good and acceptable and perfect. —Romans 12:1-2**

There is a reason the Lord is calling us to change our mind to agree with His Word. It's so we can walk in the fullness of the joy, power, and authority of His kingdom. It's so we may walk in the abundant life that He has provided for us.

But be warned, it is a process of sacrifice. A living and holy sacrifice. And it will take time.

As you continue to renew your mind, you have a sure word of promise that you will enter all that the Lord has prepared for you.

—ɯ—

Keep a journal

Your life in the Lord is a journey. It isn't a one-time event or even a series of events. It is a lifelong relationship that will grow and change over time.

I started keeping a journal in the late 1980s and haven't stopped. For the most part, my documentation consists of things directly relevant to my walk with the Lord. Here are some of the key bits of information I enter into my journal:

- Certain scriptures that stood out to me as I read them
- Things I sense the Lord is showing me through life, nature, people, or circumstances
- Questions I have or prayer requests
- Declarations of my faith
- Statements of praise and worship of my Lord
- Prophetic revelation—dreams, words of wisdom/knowledge, prophecies, etc.

It's interesting to note that most of this book could be found in my journals in one form or another.

The record of your journey is a powerful tool that will encourage and undergird you in your walk. You'll learn how to tune in to the voice of the Lord and how to be led by the Spirit. You'll come to know life-transforming truths that will guide you on the course of your life.

Yes, you'll make mistakes, encounter trials, and endure temptation. You will grow, mature, and have inspiring victories. As you record these truths, revelations, and steps in the process of growing in Christ, they'll become a profound source of strength. You will be able to reflect back on promises and see the milestones that help you discern how much you've grown.

I'm continually amazed at how the Lord will reveal something to me at one point in my life—then in the future, bring it before me again for encouragement. My journals are the most important of all my earthly possessions. It's because within those pages, I have recorded a narrative of my conversation with the Lord.

In your journey to reclaim your core and establish the foundation of your life, you will face a number of obstacles common in one degree or another among the family of the Lord. As someone who has walked this path for many years, let me share with you some things to help you remove these killers from your path.

—✷—

Reclaiming Your Core Journal
Chapter 12 Thoughts, Questions & Insights

CHAPTER 13

Removing Obstacles

When you've committed to live a healthy lifestyle and maintain physical fitness, there are certain thoughts that are best avoided. "I'd like to eat so much cake that I go into a chocolate-induced coma!" Thoughts along that line can become a huge obstacle.

Dealing with obstacles is a part of life, whether physical or spiritual. Some you have control over . . . some you don't. By eliminating the ones you can control, you'll have more strength and energy to overcome the ones you can't.

Over the years walking through the process of reclaiming the core of my faith—and helping many others do the same—I've observed many common obstacles. Often they are thoughts, ideas, and beliefs that seem logical and justifiable, but in reality, they are clever snares designed to keep us entangled in the destructive patterns of our lives.

In the truest sense of the word, they are obstacles. So take heed. Holding on to any of them will prevent you from moving forward in all that the Lord has for you.

—⟐—

The blame game

As I mentioned in the chapter regarding strongholds, one obstacle we face is getting caught up in blaming others.

Without question, many of the hurts you've experienced in life came to you at the hands of others. Often times, they were people you should have been able to trust. They were the ones who should have protected you, provided for you, and loved you.

Let me clearly state that many of the things done to you were wrong. You did not deserve to be treated that way—and no one had the right to do whatever was done to you. You are loved and worthy of love, honor, and respect.

With that being said, let me also tell you that no one has the power to determine your response to what happened other than you.

You're responsible for your response.
It's yours. You own it.
You're not a victim of what has happened to you—unless you choose to be.

Living a life of blame relegates you to a life you're unable to change. You have surrendered your life to a lie and to an event (or events) that you have no power to alter. It's not a matter of what has been done (or not done) to you. The point is, you own how you responded to it. But you can bring it to the Lord and allow Him to bring truth and healing to that area of your heart.

In no way am I suggesting this is an easy process, nor am I suggesting it won't take a significant amount of time and energy to navigate the complexities of working through the consequences of other people's action. What I am saying is that holding on to a perceived need to blame has no power to effect change and can be a huge obstacle to your growth.

Self-justification

Self-justification lives under the delusion that violating the truth of God's Word is acceptable due to the uniqueness of an individual's personal circumstances. This obstacle is one of the specific strongholds referred to in

2 Corinthians 10. It's a belief system that attempts to exalt itself above the knowledge of God—and hides behind comments like, "Well, if you went through what I've been through, you'd [fill in a deed of the flesh here] too!"

Many people in our culture of misunderstanding God's grace believe God is okay with their sinful and destructive behavior because He loves them and understands them. I can assure you, nothing could be further from the truth. If God wasn't concerned about the destructiveness of sin, He wouldn't have sent His Son to remove its power from our lives. And He wouldn't have given you His Spirit to empower you to overcome it.

The truth is that regardless of your circumstances, you will never have an adequate defense for standing in opposition to living a life led by the Spirit. Attempting to justify destructive behavior is the equivalent of arguing for your right to stay in bondage to the enemy.

—⋙—

Comparison

Comparative righteousness—*at least I'm not as bad as Bob*—and peer association—*Sue is a good person and she does it*—are not only obstacles, they are glaring indications that we don't understand the message of the gospel. The only comparison or association we're allowed to make is between Jesus Christ and ourselves. That's because He is the One we're called to conform to, and it's His life in us that we're looking to see evident in our lives.

Comparison is rooted in the idea that our righteousness is something we can attain. As we've covered at some length in previous chapters, it's clear that this isn't the case. Our righteousness was given to us, as well as to those we may be tempted to compare ourselves to. It's also important to note that only the Lord knows those areas of our lives that need addressing and in what order they need to be addressed. Just as we can trust the Lord with the process He is bringing us through, so too we can trust that He knows how to love, heal, and mature our brothers and sisters.

—⋙—

Unforgiveness

Without question, the most prevalent obstacle I've encountered in the lives of the people I have worked with is unforgiveness. Part of that is due to a misunderstanding of what forgiveness is (and isn't)—and part of it is due to a real need that we have in our hearts for justice.

This issue is much larger than what I'm able to develop here. But there are a few things you can do to help remove this obstacle from your path.

Unforgiveness is sin. Early in my life I was tormented by the memories of hurtful events that had taken place in my life. I tried and tried to forgive and forget, but the memories, the pain, and the rage continued to swell in my heart and mind. I tried numerous religious methods for forgiving—imagining the offender as a bird in a cage and letting them fly free, writing the offender a letter and burning it, etc. But nothing brought me peace.

As I cried out to the Lord, He brought me to the passage in Matthew 18:21-35, where Jesus explains the importance of forgiveness and the consequence of not giving it. I realized that I, like the wicked servant in the story, was unwilling to truly forgive even after I'd been forgiven of all my sin. The Lord clearly showed me that my judgment and unforgiveness were sin. Then He brought me to 1 John 1:9 and assured me that if I would confess my sin, He would forgive me and cleanse me.

I scheduled an appointment with a godly man I knew and asked if he would be a witness as I confessed my sin of unforgiveness. He agreed. We invited the Holy Spirit to expose every area and instance where I was holding on to that sin, and then I opened the floodgates.

For about two hours, I agreed with the Lord about every instance of anger, hate, and unforgiveness He brought to my mind. I acknowledged it was sin and received His forgiveness and cleansing of all my unrighteousness.

I don't know what the person thought of me, but it didn't matter. All I know is that I've never been the same again. I was truly free. I literally felt a hundred pounds had been lifted off of me. In that place where I'd only known hate and rage, I was completely at peace.

If you're holding on to the hurt, pains and injustices of the past (or present), agree with the Lord that it's sin. As you confess it to Him, you can accept His forgiveness and righteousness by agreeing with the truth.

Feeling pain doesn't mean you haven't forgiven. If someone comes and punches you in the face, you can forgive them—but it doesn't mean you aren't going to feel any more pain.

Working through the pain of the hurts in your life is a different process than forgiving. Even though forgiveness is the first crucial part of that process, it's only one part. Once again, working through the complexities of the healing process is too involved to give it the attention it deserves in this book, but understand that it's a separate process. You'll need to give yourself permission to walk through the emotional healing process without allowing guilt to make you think you haven't forgiven.

Many people have short-circuited the healing process. They thought that once a person was forgiven, they shouldn't think about the event any longer. Forgiveness is relinquishing the requirement of being repaid. In the process of forgiveness, we give up our right for restitution and entrust the process of justice to a loving and gracious God who will deal rightly with our offender.

Once that step has been taken, we're free to take ownership of our feelings, actions, and reactions—and ask the Lord to work through how we have responded to certain events and why.

Forgiveness isn't saying what happened is okay. Sin is sin whether it is committed by us or against us. And sin is never okay. When someone sins against me, and subsequently apologizes, I never say that it's okay. I will forgive them if needed, but I'll never condone a course of action that is outside of that which conforms to Christ. In some cases, I believe the best thing we can do for ourselves and for people perpetrating destructive behaviors is to separate ourselves from the situation or individual. Temporarily or permanently, if appropriate.

—⋙—

Keys to move beyond the obstacles

To be sure, you'll encounter these as well as other obstacles as you pursue the truth. Each of these encounters will entail the same processes we've discussed. You will identify the truth and agree with it, break agreement with the lie, align yourself in faith with the truth, and see the Lord bring you from victory to victory.

Here are a few keys to help unlock the power of the Lord so you can crush the obstacles in your path:

1. Recognize the issues you need to focus on are the obstacles in your own heart. You can do nothing to change anyone or anything other than yourself. Keep your eyes on the Lord and what He is doing in you, regardless of the circumstances you may be going through.
2. Identify the truth that exposes where your behavior is inconsistent with who the Lord says you are.
3. Ask the Holy Spirit to show you what is at the core of your behavior. Is this just the flesh or is this an old wound? Is it an issue of unrepentant sin, judgment, unforgiveness, or unfulfilled vows? Or is this an issue with your core beliefs (are you believing a lie about God, yourself, others, etc.)?
4. Review the issue from heaven's perspective. That is what the Word is talking about when it instructs us to judge with righteous judgment. God's Word will help you understand the issue from His perspective.
5. Hold on to the truth that there is no provision for the flesh in heaven (John 7:24; Romans 13:14).
6. Be quick to let go of the old way—and grab hold of the new (Ephesians 4:17-24).

Reclaiming Your Core Journal
Chapter 13 Thoughts, Questions & Insights

CHAPTER 14
Just a Word, If I May

The goal of this book is to direct your focus to the core of your faith—drawing attention to your true identity in Christ. It was written to get straight to the heart of the good news of Jesus Christ, what was provided for us through His death and resurrection. And it was written to present practical instruction on how to enter into an experiential relationship with our Father.

As such, I haven't spent much time addressing the many false or pseudo-biblical messages that have permeated our modern-day Christian culture. However, I do feel I'd be remiss in my responsibilities as a teacher if I didn't issue a few words of caution before we wrap things up.

Many of the struggles in my walk with the Lord have been a direct result of teachings that came from the church. The foundation of my faith was weakened by teachings based on scriptures taken out of context. Bits and pieces of the truth can be more destructive than total lies. The deadliest deceptions are the ones that look like the truth. Let's look at a few areas of concern.

—⁂—

Forgiveness
Don't misunderstand the purpose of your forgiveness. A price was paid to forgive you of your sins so you could become a habitation of the Holy Spirit. Jesus Christ didn't pay that debt so you could continue to sin. The

Lord made no provision for the flesh—and make no mistake, neither does He give you the right to do so. If anyone has told you that it's okay to continue living a life that willingly follows after sin, your flesh, or the ways of the world, they are lying. Don't allow yourself to be deceived.

—⚮—

Righteousness

Don't misunderstand the purpose of the gift of righteousness you were given. The righteousness of Jesus Christ was imputed to you so that you wouldn't need to waste any time trying to be something you can never be. The flesh of fallen humanity is too weak to bear the burden of righteousness. His righteousness was given so you could live a life that would be impossible any other way.

Once you accept the forgiveness of God and receive the right standing of Jesus Christ, everything that comes after that is about taking possession of what has freely been given.

It's equally important that you don't accept the lie that now that you've been born again and declared righteous, you're somehow required to maintain your own righteousness by your own effort or ability. The same old life that died to sin is the one that also died to self-righteousness. As you continue to subdue the flesh by the power of the same Spirit that raised Christ from the dead, you will walk in the new life that was given to you.

Your singular task is to be conformed to the same image of the One who now indwells you. As His son or daughter, you were designed to accomplish the good works that God prepared before the foundation of the world for you to fulfill. You'll do all of that in the strength of the life that now dwells in you.

—⚮—

Grace

There has been much discussion surrounding grace. Many are taking the word completely out of context and teaching that grace is a perpetual license to do anything you want and still be at peace with God. In order to hold to that description of grace, you must be willing to ignore the majority of God's Word.

To get a clear understanding of the meaning of grace, it's important to consider the original Greek definition as well as the context of the scriptures in which the word is used.

God's Glossary
Grace (Strong's G5463): cháris (*kha*-ris). Meaning *graciousness* (as gratifying) of manner or act—abstract or concrete, literal, figurative or spiritual, especially the divine influence upon the heart and its reflection in the life, including gratitude. Also meaning *acceptable, benefit, favor, gift, grace(-ious), joy, liberality, pleasure, thank(-s, -worthy)*.

Grace is a gift. It's a gift that imparts favor, power, and ability. Without this divine influence upon our heart, we would be unable to live a life of the Spirit.

Let me be perfectly clear. We weren't given grace so that we could continue to live after the flesh. Grace is the divine enablement to live a life empowered by and for the Spirit.

Therefore do not let sin reign in your mortal body so that you obey its lusts, and do not go on presenting the members of your body to sin as instruments of unrighteousness; but present yourselves to God as those alive from the dead, and your members as instruments of righteousness to God. For sin shall not be master over you, for you are not under law but under grace. What then? Shall we sin because we are not under law but under grace? May it never be! —Romans 6:12-15

If you've been confused by teachings on grace, I recommend doing a study of all the uses of the Greek word (identified above) throughout the book of Romans. The same word is used over 150 times in the New Testament, but the 21 times it's used in Romans will give you a good idea of the actual meaning and usage.

The Lord's grace and kindness toward us is immeasurable. Without it, you and I would have no hope. It's a powerful and amazing part of the message of the gospel—and a key truth in reclaiming your core. But just like every other key, it must work together in symphony with the sum total of God's Word.

—m—

Reclaiming Your Core Journal
Chapter 14 Thoughts, Questions & Insights

CHAPTER 15

Welcome to the Promised Land

A s you walk through the process of reclaiming your core, you'll see that much like a physical transformation, this journey takes time and persistence. Many times I've been confronted by my weakness and limitations, having to decide whether to be defined by them or press on to the goal before me.

Spiritually speaking, I'd have to say much of what I've experienced has been the removal of what has nothing to do with who I really am. This journey has been mostly the destruction of thoughts, ideas, beliefs, and behaviors that aren't a reflection of who God created me to be. As I let go of those things that weren't consistent with the truth of my identity in Christ, I've found more fruitfulness than in all my years of religious effort trying to be something I wasn't.

—⁓—

Adding to what you already have

Your participation in this world began the moment you took your first breath. As a baby, you already had everything you needed to fulfill your purpose and destiny in this life. You just had to use it and develop it.

As a new creation in Christ, you'll find the more you are free from sin and thought patterns that defeat and entangle, the more you'll be able to focus on activities that bring growth.

If you think about it, growing in Christ is a lot like building muscles. You were given your physical muscles in your mother's womb. There was nothing you did to have the muscles you now have. There is nothing you can do to obtain new muscles.

What you do with your muscles is an entirely different story. By use and by exercise you are able to increase the strength and capacity of what you already have.

There was nothing you did to be saved. Your salvation was initiated and completed by Jesus Christ before the universe was created. Your participation in what was done for you came simply by accepting it by faith. It wasn't by your works that you were born by the Spirit, any more than you were born of the flesh by your own effort. It was only by grace.

Since you now have everything you need, the only question is, what will you do with it?

You have all the muscles you'll ever have—and have the choice to use them and exercise them so they will increase. Spiritually, you have everything you need regarding how to live an abundant life filled with the Spirit, fully expressing Christ in you. The question is, will you strengthen your spiritual muscles by using everything you've been given?

—⚋—

Where to go from here

Having a strong core should be common to all believers, but each of us has been created as a unique son or daughter of our Father in heaven.

Consider how every athlete establishes and maintains a strong core, even though the expression of athletic ability is as unique as his/her personal talents, abilities, and desires.

From the basic foundations of fitness, a golfer, rock climber, football player, or Olympic athlete builds his/her body to meet the challenges inherent in the chosen sport, profession, or activity. Mostly unseen, the core enables and empowers movement in any direction—making the possibilities limitless.

As a believer, you can do anything you want with your life. Your strong core belief system and solid foundation are the basis for all that lies ahead. That life will be expressed in anything you do.

It will keep you centered and balanced.

It will steer you away from destructive behaviors.

It will infuse life and love into your relationships.

It will empower you to do amazing things.

It will lead you into the abundant life available to you in Christ.

Just like it is with your physical core, your spiritual identity may be unseen for the most part, but it's at the center of your life and will affect every movement you make.

Having a healthy core understanding of who you are that is resting on the solid foundation of your faith will also aid in the process of finding your unique expression in the body of Christ. You'll need to connect with others like you—and they will need you to connect with them. That expression is as unique as you are, so don't fall into the trap of thinking you need to be or look like anyone else.

Allow the Lord to develop your life from that place of grace in Him. You alone are responsible for exploring the depths of who you are in Christ and discovering the fullness of who you were created to be. Establishing and maintaining your strong core and solid foundation will keep you on track no matter what areas of life you explore.

From that place of being rooted and grounded in Him, the possibilities are limitless. Whether you are in ministry, education, government, the workplace, the marketplace, or media and entertainment, it doesn't matter. Your gifts and callings will grow as naturally as fruit grows on a tree.

—◊◊◊—

My wish for you

I've endeavored to salt this book with some personal examples. What I can tell you is, these few anecdotes are but a small sample of the radical change the Lord has done in my life.

The only way I would be able to begin to articulate the reality of my transformation would be to have the entire book about me. Instead of doing that, I chose to share the truths and principles that have impacted me the most.

I can tell you that my life is filled. It's an abundant life of blessings that continues to unfold around me. By employing the principles I've shared with you, I've entered into a life marked by love, joy, and peace. My marriage and relationships with my family and friends are deeper and closer than anything I have ever experienced in my life. Every year keeps getting deeper, richer, and fuller.

My wife and I have enjoyed an increasingly abundant life in Christ and have a strong desire to share it with you. This book is one step in our attempt to freely give what we've freely received.

Don't think that I'm saying that everything goes the way I want it to or that I don't have difficulties and struggles in my life. But I am saying that even in the midst of the challenges, I abide in peace.

Not only do I have my transformational testimony and that of my family's, but I also have heard the testimonies of many other individuals—people with whom the Lord has allowed me to share the same truths given in this book.

It's my sincere desire that these thoughts will help launch you forward into all our heavenly Father has for you. I pray this book helps lead you into a closer relationship with the One who loves you more than you can imagine.

May you reclaim the love, joy, and peace available to you in the Holy Spirit. May the Lord grant you freedom from anything that would slow you down in your pursuit of your core identity in Christ.

An abundant life and a profound, indescribable eternity with the Lord God of Hosts await all who hold tightly to these things until the end.

Reclaiming Your Core Journal
Chapter 15 Thoughts, Questions & Insights

Author Profile

As a pastor and minister in the body of Christ, Luke Laffin has been training and equipping believers for over three decades. He has authored articles and international missions devotionals, developed Bible-based curriculum, and maintains a blog called *The Entrance of Light* at llaffin.blogspot.com. His career has been prolific—working as an international speaker, author, teacher, life coach, as well as a professional healthcare consultant.

Luke has been growing in his relationship with God since the age of 15. Now in his 50s, he works alongside his wife, Helen, pouring into others the lessons they've learned through many heartaches, joys, challenges, victories, and failures. Luke and Helen regularly work with leaders to navigate the pressures and challenges of marriage, family, and ministry. Luke has developed and led ministry teams nationally and internationally—counseling and training many individuals throughout the years.

In 2014, Luke and Helen founded Four Winds Global Foundation to help individuals discover their true identity, purpose, and passion in Christ.

As much as possible, Luke and Helen spend time with their children and grandchildren living in various parts of the country. They also pursue a healthy lifestyle and enjoy working out together—completing two Spartan Race events since turning 50.

Made in the USA
Middletown, DE
13 July 2017